Ghetto Revolts

Trans-action Books

Ghetto Revolts

Edited by
PETER H. ROSSI

Trans- **action** Books

Published by
Aldine Publishing Company

The essays in this book originally appeared
in *Trans-* **action** Magazine

HV
6477
R67

Contents

Preface

However diverse their attitudes and interpretations may sometimes be, social scientists are now entering a period of shared realization that the United States—both at home and abroad—has entered a crucial period of transition. Indeed, the much burdened word "crisis" has now become a commonplace among black militants, Wall Street lawyers, housewives, and even professional politicians.

For the past seven years, *Trans*-action magazine has dedicated itself to the task of reporting the strains and conflicts within the American system. But the magazine has done more than this. It has pioneered in social programs for changing the society, offered the kind of analysis that has permanently restructured the terms of the "dialogue" between peoples and publics, and offered the sort of prognosis that makes for real alterations in social and political policies directly affecting our lives.

The work done in the pages of *Trans*-action has crossed

professional boundaries. This represents much more than simple cross-disciplinary "team efforts." It embodies rather a recognition that the social world cannot be easily carved into neat academic areas. That, indeed, the study of the experience of blacks in American ghettos, or the manifold uses and abuses of agencies of law enforcement, or the sorts of overseas policies that lead to the celebration of some dictatorships and the condemnation of others, can best be examined from many viewpoints and from the vantage points of many disciplines.

This series of books clearly demonstrates the superiority of starting with real world problems and searching out practical solutions, over the zealous guardianship of professional boundaries. Indeed, it is precisely this approach that has elicited enthusiastic support from leading American social scientists for this new and dynamic series of books.

The demands upon scholarship and scientific judgment are particularly stringent, for no one has been untouched by the current situation. Each essay republished in these volumes bears the imprint of the author's attempt to communicate his own experience of the crisis. Yet, despite the sense of urgency these papers exhibit, the editors feel that many have withstood the test of time, and match in durable interest the best of available social science literature. This collection of *Trans*-action articles, then, attempts to address itself to immediate issues without violating the basic insights derived from the classical literature in the various fields of social science.

The subject matter of these books concern social changes that have aroused the long-standing needs and present-day anxieties of us all. These changes are in organizational life styles, concepts of human ability and intelligence, changing patterns of norms and morals, the relationship of social conditions to physical and biological environments, and in the status of social science with national policy making.

The dissident minorities, massive shifts in norms of social conduct, population explosions and urban expansions, and vast realignments between nations of the world of recent years do not promise to disappear in the seventies. But the social scientists involved as editors and authors of this *Trans*-action series have gone beyond observation of these critical areas, and have entered into the vital and difficult tasks of explanation and interpretation. They have defined issues in a way making solutions possible. They have provided answers as well as asked the right questions. Thus, this series should be conceived as the first collection dedicated not to hightlighting social problems alone, but to establishing guidelines for social solutions based on the social sciences.

THE EDITORS
Trans-action

Introduction

PETER H. ROSSI

Despite revolutionary beginnings and an almost fatal experience with a major civil war, Americans have adopted a political rhetoric which avoids the domestic use of such terms as "revolt," "rebellion" and "revolution." A naive reader of conventional American secondary school texts almost needs a decoding device to translate "The War of Independence" as revolution against British rule and the "War Between the States" as the unsuccessful revolt of the Deep South. The blandness of conventional American political rhetoric is even more apparent when we consider the terms in which the events of more recent times are discussed: The revolts of urban black ghettos in the 1960s have been made semantically more palatable by being called "civil disorders," almost as if the body politic were suffering from some temporary stomach upset.

Yet there is more than semantic pollyannaism in the use

1

of "civil disorders." The ghetto uprisings were not revolutionary in the sense of being organized to attain articulated political goals. But they were more than civil disorders in the sense of being more than crowds which, for some reason or another, the police were unable to control; that would put them on a par with the spring vacation gatherings of youths in Fort Lauderdale that overwhelm the local and state police and cause incidental damage to property. The 1960s events in the ghettos were large-scale collective actions involving wholesale defiance of established authority and violation of established property relationships. They were truly revolts, arising out of deeply felt feelings of inequitable deprivation and expressing alienation from the larger society, its values, and its official representatives. Yet the revolts were not entirely revolutionary, for they took place without formal leadership or articulated revolutionary ideology, more like wildcat strikes than planned and sustained work stoppages.

The ghetto revolts of the 1960s had modest beginnings. A few small disturbances in 1963 and 1964 received some attention in the national press. Some places, like Rochester, New York and Chicago were disturbed by what appeared to be unusual levels of unrest in their ghettos. But ghetto revolts only really moved to the center stage of national attention in 1965 with the uprising in the Watts area of Los Angeles. From 1965 in Watts to the Spring of 1968, city after city in the urban North experienced more or less extensive revolts in one or more of its black ghettos. None of the major metropolitan areas in the North and West escaped some form of ghetto revolt. In some cities—Detroit and Newark are best examples—the battles beween ghetto blacks and the local authorities went so badly against the latter that the military establishment had to be called to re-establish order. In other cities—for example, San Francisco and Minneapolis—the revolts were brief and easy for local authorities to bring under control. In all cities, however, the scars of the revolts are still evident: in some places, in the still standing gutted buildings and boarded up stores; in others, in a residual atmosphere of nervous apprehension. The remains of the major revolts are still visible: The main commercial strip in Watts has yet to be rebuilt and Washington D.C.'s 14th Street is dotted with empty lots paved with rubble and stores blackened by fire and still boarded up.

The Watts revolt was a great shock to white America. The first response was to strive to understand what happened and to search for the specific cause that triggered the events of August 1965. Investigators, including some social scientists, swarmed over Watts to determine what had happened. They found that an incident involving the police had marked the beginning of the revolt. The investigators also found that those who participated in the revolt were no different from the average resident of Watts except by being younger and more likely to be male: The revolt was not started and sustained by criminal elements—quite the contrary. Governor Brown appointed a former head of the Central Intelligence Agency to chair a commission which reported these facts and attended primarily to the kinds of police tactics which would be necessary to counter the spread of similar uprisings in the future. (See the perceptive review of this document by Robert S. Blauner "Whitewash over Watts" *Trans*-action, March-April, 1966.)

The McCone Commission found that Watts was a deprived area, high on all the indicators of depressed social conditions (unemployment, poor housing, inadequate municipal services, poor medical and social services and so forth). These disclosures were hardly news to social scientists who had been keeping track of black progress (or lack of it) in the United States.

The response of public officials was to augment the social services of Watts and to devise new training experiences for the police. The Office of Economic Opportunity took Watts on as a special project and programs began to appear on the scene (manpower retraining, a neighborhood health center) that had until then passed over the area.

1966 saw additional ghetto revolts. A small-scale flareup, again in Watts, was followed by more serious revolts in Chicago and in the Hough area of Cleveland. The Kerner Commission's report counted 43 disorders and riots for that year, most on a very small scale.

The longest hot summer was that of 1967: Tampa, Florida erupted in June to be followed within a few days by Cincinnati and Atlanta. But these disorders were to be overshadowed by the prolonged revolts in Newark and Detroit. Each was to engage the attention of the nation for more than a week and to present television viewers with views of billowing smoke, looters, gutted stores and dwellings. Following Newark, a serious revolt broke out in Plainfield, New Jersey, and in a number of northern New Jersey cities outbreaks were narrowly averted. Following Detroit, revolts broke out in the black ghettos of a half a dozen Michigan cities.

When the summer of 1967 came to an end, the nation was in shock. Although attention was centered on the major revolts in Newark and Detroit, 164 "disturbances" in 1967 were counted by the Kerner Commission, of which eight were serious enough to involve calling in military forces. Every section of the country was represented in the tally, although the East and Midwest experienced seven of the eight serious ones.

Shortly after Detroit had been restored to some semblance of normality President Johnson appointed Governor Otto Kerner to head up a *National Advisory Commission on Civil Disorders*. In a frenzy of activity, ably described in the article by Lipsky and Olson in this volume, the Kerner Commission issued its famous *Report* in March 1968. More than a million and a half copies of the report were sold in a paperback edition issued by a commercial publisher. The *Report* has become a standard source, to be referred to authoritatively in discussions of the position of blacks in this country, and is acknowledged as such by both blacks and whites.

It was only six weeks after the *Report* was issued that the last major round of revolts occurred. Sparked by the assassination of Dr. Martin Luther King, Jr., major revolts broke out in Washington, D.C., Baltimore, Pittsburgh and Chicago and minor "disturbances" occurred in more than a score of other urban communities. By the end of 1968 every major northern city had experienced at least one serious ghetto revolt. All cities nervously awaited the summer of 1969.

But the summer of 1969 was a relatively peaceful one. A score of minor incidents occurred in the major cities, with some serious revolts occurring in such smaller places as Lancaster, Pennsylvania. The nation began to breath a sigh of relief, with the thought that maybe the revolts were over.

Looking at decades before the sixties, it is clear that race relations in the urban North have never been particularly peaceful. The Draft Riots in New York City during the Civil War ended with mobs sacking the Negro sections of the city and attacking its inhabitants. The influx of blacks into the urban centers during World War I and in the early twenties was accompanied by race riots, notably in Chicago and East Saint Louis. During the 1920s heyday of the Klu Klux Klan in

Indiana, Ohio and Illinois, blacks were driven out of many of the smaller cities in those states. Early in World War II, the population of Harlem took over the streets, smashing property and looting on 125th Street and Lenox Avenue. In 1943, the Detroit race riot led city fathers to call on federal troops to break up a mass confrontation between Detroit whites and blacks. Other major cities like Chicago and New York nervously made preparations for heightened black-white tensions during the same period.

But the revolts of the sixties were different. First of all, unlike the race riots that followed World War I and World War II, the revolts were not mass confrontations of blacks and whites. The typical race riot of the earlier period involved a dispute between whites and blacks over rights of residence in or usage of pieces of urban territory: The 1919 Chicago riot started over customary usage of bathing beaches on Lake Michigan. Almost without exception, the riots of the 1960s involved only blacks and law enforcement agents. Blacks did not attempt to move out of their neighborhoods and the few scattered attempts by whites to enter black ghettos were turned back by the police and troops. The revolts of the sixties were directed towards the police and toward property.

Secondly, the riots were not local phenomena. It was easy to develop evidence for a theory of local determinism up through 1966, but when the revolts spread to every major city, it became increasingly clear that the particularities of any city were irrelevant. Thus the Kerner Commission started out with the theory that it would be possible to explain why "civil disorders" occurred in some but not in other cities on the basis of the level of local grievance in relation to the responsiveness of local government administrations to those grievances. Such a theory seemed to account for the occurrences in such illiberal cities as Chicago, Los Angeles and Newark, but it was hard to describe either New York or Detroit (or, later on, Baltimore, Washington and Pittsburgh) as governed by mayors and city administrations who were insensitive to their black constituents. Furthermore, the quick spread of revolts from Newark to other Northern New Jersey cities and from Detroit to other Michigan places was additional evidence for a nonlocal interpretation of the revolts.

Finally, the disorders occurred in a period when the objective position of the blacks was not in a precipitous decline. The War on Poverty had been declared by President Johnson and Congress in 1964. By 1965, manpower retraining programs, The Job Corps, Community Action Programs, Head Start and the like were all underway. The Civil Rights Act of 1964 had also been one of the first acts of the Johnson succession, legislation which was actively being enforced by the Justice Department under Robert Kennedy. It was true that no dramatic improvements in the conditions of blacks in urban ghettos had resulted, but was it fair to expect dramatic improvements with just a year's trial run?

These considerations led the Kerner Commission to look for the roots of the riots in the longstanding conditions of urban blacks. "Centuries of neglect," the heritage of "white racism," widespread discrimination became the basic causes in the Kerner Commission *Report* with some blame placed on local police and local administrations for insensitive handling of the police actions taken to counter the revolts once started. In the minds of many Americans, the theme of white racism stands out as the major message of the Kerner Commission report concerning the root causes of the civil disorders of the 1960s. (Yet the term white racism occurs very infrequently in the *Report* itself. It was mentioned several times in the summary—written by Lindsay's aides, according to Lipsky—only once or twice in the body of the *Report,* but accented heavily in Tom Wicker's introduction to the Bantam Books paperback edition.)

As a causal factor white racism is at best a truism; at worst a theory that can lead one down many fruitless paths. It is obvious that at minimum a large part of the blame for the conditions under which southern and northern blacks live lies in the fact that white Americans have systematically and thoroughly discriminated against them in almost every area of social life. However, it is not clear what follows in the way of social policy from this fact. Does it mean that amelioration of the conditions of blacks will have to wait for the demise of white racism? How does one go about getting rid of white racism?

It is true that black militants found the phrase white racism quite useful both as an accusation to hurl at whites of every spectrum of political opinion and as a cry around which to rally their black constituents. It is also true that whites found this single factor useful as well, perhaps because by purging themselves as individuals they could delude themselves into thinking that they have made their major contribution to the solution of the plight of American blacks. Despite these utilitarian aspects, as a cause of revolts, white racism has led both blacks and whites astray.

As an explanation, white racism fails in two important respects: First, it points to a very general condition and contains within itself very little indication as to what specific social policies ought to be followed to remedy the condition. Secondly, it draws attention away from the meaning of the revolts—what were ghetto residents expressing in undertaking the revolts? It is true that it is both hard to understand what are the implicit goals of instances of collective behavior like the ghetto revolts and it is also true that it is not easy to lay out the programs of social policy that will both reduce the underlying longstanding conditions and satisfy the barely articulated goals of the blacks who revolted. Nevertheless, these are the tasks that are essential to undertake.

Perhaps the most significant fact about the revolts of the 1960s was their ubiquitousness. Liberal and conservative city administrations alike faced revolts in their ghettos. So did cities which had small proportions of blacks and cities which had large proportions of blacks. Ghetto blacks all over the urban North were alike in expressing their discontent with their lot by engaging in revolts. Whatever blacks were expressing in their revolts, it was common to all cities.

Furthermore, since none of the investigations were able to find that the revolts were led either by individuals or by organizations, the purpose to be sought seemed to be those which are individual in character rather than collective. The revolts look as if large numbers of individuals suddenly all begin to behave in much the same way, innocuous enough when it is an instance of many people putting up their umbrellas in response to a shower, but overwhelming when it is an instance of masses of people suddenly rejecting the authority of law enforcement officials and the usual rules governing use of property. It is clear that the revolts were more than a case of a large number of individuals suddenly engaging in the same sorts of behavior. The revolts are expressions that challenge the legitimacy of existing authority and institutions: in defying the police and looting commercial establishments, ghetto blacks suddenly expressed attitudes which they held all along, to the effect that local institutions were not of their making, were inimicable to their interests and had a legitimacy only by virtue of definitions which they did not share.

The revolts therefore bore the message that the mass of urban blacks were alienated from their local communities and from the larger society. It was a message repeated from place to place and passed on from ghetto to ghetto. Only in those cities in which blacks could anticipate massive reprisals were there no revolts. For example, in Jersey City the police chief is reputed to have passed the word to ghetto leaders that an outbreak of rioting would bring the police out shooting. Similarly, a revolt in Alabama or Mississippi, (or for that matter any city in Georgia other than Atlanta) would bring about reprisals so severe that it would be almost suicidal.

The consequences of the urban revolts of the sixties are still being shaped. The immediate reactions of the federal agencies and the local city administrations were to push forward their efforts to ameliorate the conditions of blacks. The War on Poverty did not slacken until in 1969 the war in Vietnam began to eat into funds for all domestic programs. Local city administrations attempted somehow to establish contact with the ghetto, giving rise in some places to a frenzied scramble among putative black leaders for the new vacancies in the roster of recognized black representatives.

Perhaps the most important consequences of the revolts were political in character. Black communities all over the country are becoming more and more organized. The revolts were a manifestation of power and solidarity and indicated what could be accomplished if blacks massed their individual political powers into collective action. The new poverty and related agencies provided jobs for black leaders. Out of the combination of leaders and expressed needs new urban "machines" are being constructed.

At the same time the consciousness of being black was heightened in the urban ghettos. Militant blacks extolled an ideology in which black was at least as beautiful as white. Blacks were on their way to becoming an American ethnic group, conscious and proud of their cultural identity, and willing to act collectively on the political front.

The heightened social and political consciousness of blacks, however, was not without its negative consequences. Lower middle-class whites began to see that the attention given to blacks meant that less attention was given to their needs and demands. If blacks achieved more attention from local and national political leaders, then such attention was bought to some degree at their expense. Furthermore, policies aimed at improving the position of blacks economically, politically and residentially were often achieved at the expense of some deprivation of working class whites. Thus it was all very well for upper middle-class white liberals to advocate the hiring of more blacks in high level blue collar occupations, but that meant that some jobs were to be taken away from blue collar whites. Similarly policies aimed at achieving residential or school integration meant that working-class neighborhoods and working-class schools were going to be integrated.

The backlash of white discontent began to be discerned increasingly in the urban North. It manifested itself in the support given to George Wallace in the 1968 presidential campaign, and in the hard political struggles for the mayoralty in Los Angeles, New York, Cleveland and Detroit. It can be expected to grow in importance as a political factor in local and national politics in the coming years.

What of the future? Can we expect more ghetto revolts? What is the political future of the white working-class backlash?

As the ghetto becomes more and more organized with political and parapolitical organizations claiming more and more of the allegiance of ghetto blacks we can anticipate that the revolts will decline in frequency. A revolt is an inefficient political device compared to more disciplined and more focused political demonstrations of strength. As black leaders emerge and press their demands on local administrations and national officials, the political messages will become clearer and the accompanying manifestations of collective strength will become more coherent.

At the same time we can expect that as the political strength of urban blacks grows so will the strength of the white backlash. Whether or not the political struggle for better conditions for blacks is in fact a zero-sum game with working class whites as the other players, it is certain to be seen as such by working class whites. This development may mean at one extreme that the "civil disorders" of the 1970s will be communal riots in which masses of whites and blacks will confront each other in guerilla-like warfare on the streets. On a lesser level, it may mean the replacement of liberal mayors who have been responsive to black demands with "law and order" mayors who are pledged to hold the line on the urban ghetto, a tactic which may only radicalize further the political development of blacks. The 1970s may be an interesting period to view from the perspective of a future historian, but for those of us who will have to live through the decade it will be fraught with perils for the political fabric of our society and bodes ill for social peace within our major urban areas.

Cleveland's Crisis Ghetto

WALTER WILLIAMS

The riot in the Hough section of Cleveland, Ohio, occurred in July 1966. Not much more than a year earlier, in April 1965, the Bureau of the Census had conducted a special census for Cleveland that showed unexpected social and economic changes in the five years since 1960. What was most significant was a sharp economic polarization among the city's Negroes. A substantial number had moved up to a more affluent life; but the group in the worst part of the ghetto was at a level of poverty that was actually *below* the one recorded in 1960. Who rose and who stayed behind, and why?

What is most startling about the changes revealed by Cleveland's special census is their magnitude. These five years saw rapidly rising real income and falling unemployment for the city as a whole—but not for the very poor. The gap between haves and have-nots widened strikingly; and the most rapid widening was among Negroes—between those outside the slums who were rising, beginning finally to cash in on the American dream, and those still in the hard-core ghetto, on limited rations of income and hope.

In the special census nine neighborhoods at the bottom economically were grouped together and called the "Neighborhood." (See map.) The rest of the city, in which the prospering middle and upper classes are concentrated, was called the "Remainder of Cleveland." In Cleveland, however—as in the Inferno—there are different levels on the path downward, and one area of the Neighborhood is especially bad. This is the "Crisis Ghetto." It is predominantly Negro. Hough is part of it—on the edge.

The group that rose most swiftly in the period 1960-1965 were the Negroes who did not live in the Neighborhood. In 1960 they numbered 22,000. By 1965 their number had almost doubled. In all Cleveland they had achieved the greatest economic gains, showing that the door of opportunity, for some at least, was opening wider. (And also providing a convenient, but unwarranted, rationalization against help for the less fortunate—for if some Negroes could rise so quickly through their own efforts, why not all?)

At the opposite end of Cleveland's economic spectrum we find a grim picture. The number of Negro children in poor female-headed households increased sharply. By 1965 nearly two-thirds of these poor Negro youths in female families were in the Crisis Ghetto. Further, the Crisis Ghetto's average resident was in worse economic straits than in 1960. Unemployment was higher, income lower, and a larger percentage of the population was poor.

In relative terms the Crisis Ghetto was further away from the rest of the city than in 1960 in terms of major economic indices. For instance, the income gap between the Crisis Ghetto and the next economic stratum (the other

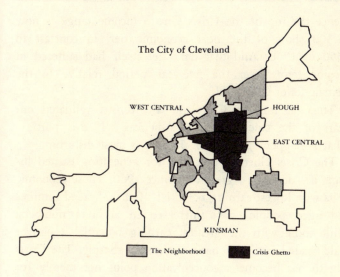

The City of Cleveland

WEST CENTRAL

HOUGH

EAST CENTRAL

KINSMAN

The Neighborhood   Crisis Ghetto

five sections of the Neighborhood) had spread visibly. The range of median real incomes for the four sections of the Crisis Ghetto and the five sections in the rest of the neighborhood was as follows:

Range of Median Incomes	1960	1965
Crisis Ghetto	$3,170-4,900	$3,000-4,160
Rest of Neighborhood	$5,450-6,230	$5,460-6,500

Hence the top of the Crisis Ghetto income range is now $1,300 short of the next economic tier, in contrast to $550 in 1960. And that next tier itself had suffered in income terms over the five-year period relative to the Remainder of Cleveland.

Thus, at least in Cleveland, the census validated our fears of the emerging "two Americas." If this portrays what is happening in other cities, it is most disturbing.

The Crisis Ghetto's potential for generating earned income has declined a great deal since 1960. Those economic units with lowest earning potential—female-headed families and aged people—have increased in absolute numbers, while those with the greatest earning potential (younger male-headed families) have diminished sharply. The Crisis Ghetto has become a concentration point not merely for the poor, but for the hard-core poor—those with least hope or opportunity of being anything else.

The increasing distance between Cleveland's majority and its disadvantaged segment is frequently hidden in the overall economic indices of the city. Averaging the increasingly prosperous and the stable poor seems to give a "rise" to everybody. But the almost unchanged poverty rate between 1960 and 1965 masks within different groups large movements that have further split the population. Between 1960 and 1965, the poverty rate:

—declined markedly among male-headed families while it increased among female-headed families;

—fell for white people, but remained almost unchanged for Negroes;

—yet showed a much greater decline (almost 40 percent below the 1960 level) for non-Neighborhood Negroes than for any other group (the whites outside the Neighborhood experienced a 12 percent decrease);

—and rose sharply in the Crisis Ghetto while it fell in the Remainder of Cleveland.

Another important change was in the *kinds* of poor families and poor people in the Crisis Ghetto. Between 1960 and 1965, the number of poor people fell by roughly 14,000. But members of Negro female-headed families increased by almost 12,000 persons (all but the merest handful of whom were found in the Neighborhood) while persons in families headed by Negro males and white males and females decreased by 26,000. As a consequence of these population changes in the five-year period, members of Negro female-headed families increased from one-fifth to one-third of Cleveland's poor. And in 1965, 60 percent of these poor, Negro, female-headed family members lived in the Crisis Ghetto.

Changes in the structure of industry have hurt the Crisis Ghetto. As Louis Buckley notes in discussing the plight of the low-skilled city laborer:

The changes in the demand for labor in our central cities have been in the direction of expansions of industries requiring well educated white collar workers and a relative decline in the industries employing blue collar unskilled and semi-skilled workers.

Many of these modern industries have fled to the suburbs. Unfortunately, public transportation has not followed, so ghetto residents have difficulty getting out to suburban jobs.

Further, an increasing percentage of the Crisis Ghetto's residents are in families whose heads have the least likelihood of increasing materially their earned income. In general, the two groups with the most limited economic potential are family units (our definition of unit includes single persons living alone) headed by women and by the aged. These groups rose significantly over the five-year period as a percentage of the Crisis Ghetto population. Not only do these two groups seem *least* likely to earn much more than at present—but they seem the *most* likely group to suffer an actual as well as a relative decline in earned income. In short, they have the lowest chance to improve their financial position, and the highest probability of declining. Once a unit in this limited potential group becomes poor, by definition, it is likely to remain so. This persistent poverty is the eroding evil. Real income in the Crisis Ghetto declined by 2 percent for male-headed families and 15 percent for female-headed families between 1960 and 1965. At the end of the five-year period unemployment rates for both men (14.6 percent) and women (17.2 percent—up over one-third since 1960) were higher, standing at nearly three times the city's average; and the poverty level had risen from 36 to 40 percent. In 1965 the average Crisis Ghetto inhabitant was worse off than he had been in 1960, both absolutely and relative to others in the city. (The pattern of deterioration is shown in the tables.)

These facts have major implications. On the one hand, those with economic strength or potential *can* flee the Crisis Ghetto. (True, if Negro, they may only be allowed to escape to a better Negro area.) But is is also clear that entrapment in the Crisis Ghetto springs directly from poverty. The price over the wall is primarily money, not

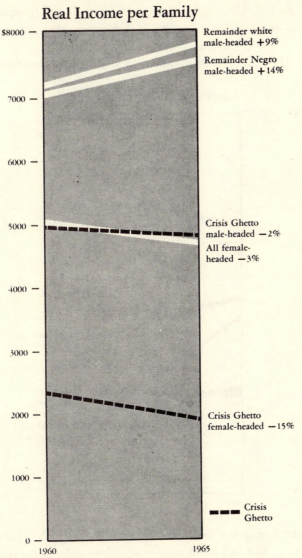

Real Income per Family

$8000

Remainder white
male-headed +9%

Remainder Negro
male-headed +14%

7000

6000

5000

Crisis Ghetto
male-headed −2%

All female-
headed −3%

4000

3000

2000

Crisis Ghetto
female-headed −15%

1000

Crisis
Ghetto

0

1960   1965

skin color. However, once poverty has locked one into the Crisis Ghetto, the chances of being forced to remain—and the bad consequences of remaining—are greater than if one lived in any other area of the city.

The Crisis Ghetto population declined by about 20 per-

Unemployment Rates

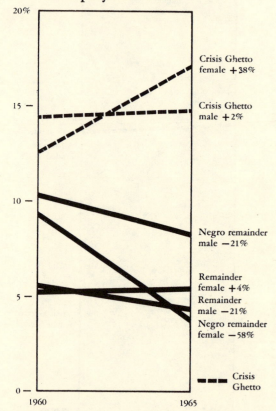

cent during the five years (from 170,000 to 134,000 persons), and this exodus might seem to imply an explanation for the decline and the change. After all, if the more able, above-average people leave, averages should move down.

But exodus, by itself, cannot explain enough. Certainly the population decrease cannot be used to explain the absolute *increases* since 1960 of a few hundreds in the number of female-headed families, and of some 3,000 poor persons in such families. Yet that is what happened; and we have no pat explanation for it.

Nor does the population decrease necessarily counter-balance the possible adverse effects coming from the declining economic situation, particularly the rise in weak economic units as a part of the total population. These people seem likely to face the Crisis Ghetto over an extended period of time. What are the consequences?

The deleterious effects of a hard-core ghetto spread beyond the economy to the total environment—to schools, to street associations, to the preservation of life itself. This last point was driven home when three Washington medical schools threatened to pull out of the D.C. General Hospital because the meager budget provided almost medieval services. Even to be sick in the Crisis Ghetto is far more dangerous than in the suburbs. So, from birth to death the ghetto marks each person, and cuts his chances either to escape or survive. The Crisis Ghetto lacks the precise boundaries and imposed restrictions of the European ghettos of the past; but it is, nevertheless, an existing reality that limits and blights the lives of its inhabitants as effectively as did the old ghettos and pales.

Is this pattern confined to Cleveland? Only in Cleveland was a special census made for the city as a whole. But figures available for 1960-65 for South Los Angeles (which includes Watts and in an economic sense is like the Cleveland Neighborhood) also show a decrease in real income per family, a small increase in the percent of poor people,

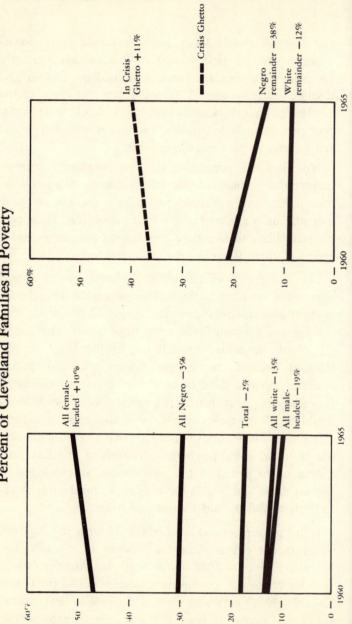

Percent of Cleveland Families in Poverty

In Crisis Ghetto +11%

Crisis Ghetto

Negro remainder —38%

White remainder —12%

60%
50
40
30
20
10
0

1960   1965

All female-headed +10%

All Negro —3%

Total —2%

All white —13%
All male-headed —19%

60%
50
40
30
20
10
0

1960   1965

and a decrease in the male and increase in female unemployment rates (the Crisis Ghetto differs only in that it shows a very small male unemployment increase). Further, Negro female family members became a far more significant proportion of South Los Angeles poor (we do not have city-wide data) increasing from 37 percent to 48 percent. While the number of poor people in Negro female-headed households rose by 9,500 (roughly 25 percent) the number of poor among white male, white female, and Negro male-headed families all decreased.

At the national level poor Negro female-headed family members have increased both absolutely and as a proportion of the total poor population. For 1960 and 1966, the number of poor persons (in millions) for these categories was as follows: (Data furnished by Mollie Orshansky.)

	1960		1966	
	Number in millions	% of total poor	Number in millions	% of total poor
Negro female-headed family members	3.2	8%	3.8	12%
All other poor persons	35.7	92	28.9	88
Total poor persons	38.9	100	32.7	100

The non-Neighborhood Negro has advanced greatly in the five years between the two censuses—more, as noted, than any other Cleveland group. Of course, this great improvement can be partly explained by residential segregation. The white on the rise goes to the suburbs—and out of the Cleveland census area—while his Negro counterpart must stay in the city. Still, there is no doubt that the Negroes escaping the Neighborhood are advancing as a group more rapidly than any within the city limits, and closing in on the Remainder of Cleveland whites. Even more striking than their increasing prosperity were their increasing numbers—from 22,000 to 41,000. They now account for 15 percent of the Negro population.

The Cleveland data indicate that economic discrimination has declined in Cleveland since 1960. Is this only in the upper and middle level jobs or has discrimination lessened across the board? I believe it may have lessened somewhat across the board; but this may not help the Crisis Ghetto Negroes unless direct action is taken to overcome their difficulties. Any decrease in overt economic discrimination, of course, is encouraging. However, it is absurd to think that this change *alone*—even if the reduction in discrimination had been far greater than I expect it was in Cleveland— will set right all the damage of the past. The liabilities of the Crisis Ghetto Negroes caused by past discrimination —poor education, lack of skills, poor health, police records —would still hold them back in the job market. In fact, the reduction in discrimination *alone* may exacerbate the split between the various strata of Cleveland Negroes.

Earlier discrimination possibly served as a lid for the advancement of *all* Negroes, squeezing them closer together in income and opportunity despite differences in skills and potentials. But once the lid was lifted, especially during boom years, the more skilled, educated, and able rose much more rapidly than the others. So the gap widened. Unless something is done the more able Negroes should continue to widen their lead until they too become part of the symbols of success that have so far evaded the Crisis Ghetto Negroes and make failure ever more visible and disturbing.

At the opposite pole, though population in the Crisis Ghetto declined by one-fifth, Negro female-headed families increased by 8 percent, children in these families by 25 percent (16,900 to 21,000), and children in *poor* Negro female-headed families by 30 percent (13,100 to 17,000). Of the 21,000 children of female-headed families in the Crisis Ghetto, 17,000 are living below the poverty level. And it is this increasing group of female-headed families that suffered the largest real income decline of the five-year period, falling from $2,300 to $1,950 per family per year. That is, at the later survey date (1965), the average Crisis Ghetto female-headed family had an income *per week* of just over $37.50.

The implications of these statistics are appalling. There were 3,900 *more* poverty-stricken children in the ghetto in 1965 than 1960—in a population 36,000 less—and there is no reason to believe that this trend is not continuing or accelerating. These children can do least to improve their condition—yet they must have a tremendous influence on the future of the Neighborhood, and of all Cleveland.

Poor Negro children in female-headed families are the great tragedy of the Crisis Ghetto. They constitute 13 percent of all persons there, 30 percent of all the children. They make up over half of the members of the poor limited-potential families.

There has been tremendous movement in and out of the Crisis Ghetto—at least four out of every ten departed or died in the five years. But the option of movement is not a random phenomenon affecting all equally. It seems available at will to some and almost completely closed to others—and most tightly closed to adults with limited economic potential, and their children.

Although the percentage of people with limited economic potential in the Crisis Ghetto is about twice as large as the population in the Remainder of Cleveland, the percentage of poor among them—standing at nearly 25 percent—is about *five* times as large. (See tables.)

Recent prosperity has removed many from the rolls of the needy, but those remaining may be far more discon-

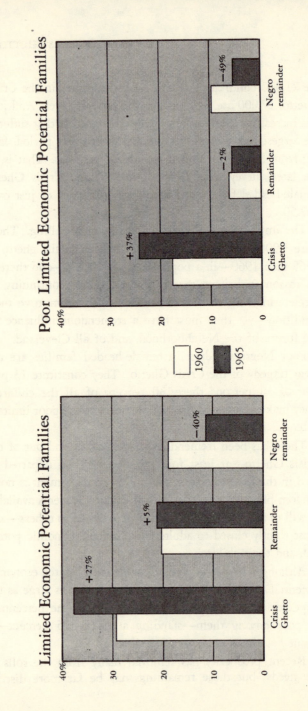

Limited Economic Potential Families

Crisis Ghetto: +27%
Remainder: +5%
Negro remainder: −40%

1960
1965

Poor Limited Economic Potential Families

Crisis Ghetto: +37%
Remainder: −2%
Negro remainder: −49%

tented than when most of their neighbors were also poor. "Relative deprivation" is a very real force. For example, the classic study of this phenomenon made during World War II showed that there was more jealousy and dissatisfaction in an Air Force fighter squadron noted for rapid promotions ("boy colonels") than in a military police unit with few promotions. This feeling of being ignored, discriminated against, and isolated, while all around others rise, may create a far more explosive situation than when many are in the same boat, as during the Depression.

The Cleveland Census reveals the city's contrasting prosperity and decay. Sharp differences emerge within the Negro population. The rapid income increase for non-Neighborhood Negroes probably indicates less economic discrimination. Also, while residential segregation remained strong, the white flight to the suburbs opened up some of the desirable Cleveland residential areas. For example, Lee Miles, an area with many expensive dwellings, changed from 28 to 72 percent Negro in five years (21,000 Negroes by 1965). Many strong economic units fled the ghetto.

As many fled to better circumstances, others became more ensnarled. And by 1965 the most disadvantaged group had grown to a very significant portion of the total Crisis Ghetto population. Particularly depressing is the increase of poor Negro young people in the economically weak female-headed homes—young people whose bondage becomes more oppressive as the rest of the city grows more prosperous.

What can be done? What can be our long term goals?

The ghetto male, frequently with limited skills, enters the job market with grave liabilities. Often the job does not pay him enough to support his family and has little prospect of leading to a living wage. The longer the man works, the longer he fails as a provider. His marriage will frequently deteriorate. As Elliot Liebow has suggested in *Tally's Corner,* the unprovided-for family becomes a continuous symbol of a man's inability to fulfill the demands of his society—to be a man. So he opts out, and the sparse existence of the female-headed family has begun.

Job and training programs for men in the Crisis Ghetto are thus a first order need. Employment that yields a living wage over time seems to be the best bet for *preventing* family break-up, and *re-establishing* stable families.

Many broken homes, however, are not going to be re-established. Consequently, the female-headed family, as the Cleveland data show so starkly, will face a particularly exposed financial position. The mother may well seek a relationship with a man that has some prospect of offering family stability and also additional income. Unfortunately, the "eligible" males are often the failures from prior marriages. The woman enters a tenuous relationship with the very unrealistic hope that it will work into a real family situation. The result is often another child.

Programs thus must be aimed at providing greater economic stability to the female-headed family. Job programs should be readily accessible for women as well as men. This means that major efforts for establishing day care centers are needed. Yet, work is not the answer for all these women. Also needed are better programs of income maintenance which will provide the family a reasonable income.

It is clear that our long run goals should be to prevent the breakup of families. But, many families are beyond the prevention of this sort. Further, the Negro mother has shown remarkable strength as a family head. Her great weakness has been in producing sufficient income, and the resultant poverty has had an adverse effect on the family.

If these deficiencies can be overcome by work or transfer income, many of these mothers may be able to properly motivate their children. If freed from poverty, the inner strength of the matriarchal Negro family may begin to assert a positive effect upon the Crisis Ghetto.

Income increases from work and transfer payments are vital, but I believe that we must go beyond income programs to effect basic institutional changes in both the larger community that includes the Crisis Ghetto and the ghetto itself. A city must provide adequate education, health, and other services for all its residents. Further, direct community action must help Crisis Ghetto residents end the growing social decay in that area. As Richard A. Cloward and Lloyd E. Ohlin observed in *Delinquency and Opportunity,* the hard-core ghetto community must be structured to provide both social control and legitimate avenues of social ascent. That is, the neighborhood community—the Crisis Ghetto—must be a sound base of opportunity. The resident of the Crisis Ghetto must be able to form a realistic belief in a decent life.

We see the alternative in current trends. The poor in the Crisis Ghetto are falling further behind. Not only distance is building up between the two poles, but tension as well—as with electrodes approaching a sparking point.

If what is happening in Cleveland is also happening in other cities, we must multiply this tension, and the danger signals, by a large factor. If by inaction we consign the misery of the parents in the Crisis Ghettos to their children, the sickness of the central cities must fester and grow worse. Hough may be a pale prelude to other, greater Houghs—a short dramatic prologue, announcing that the tragedy has begun.

September 1967

FURTHER READING SUGGESTED BY THE AUTHOR:

Tally's Corner by Elliot Liebow (Boston: Little, Brown, & Co., 1967). An anthropological field study of Negro street-corner men which seems relevant to the study of family formation by females.

Negroes in the Cities by Karl E. Taeuber and Alma F. Taeuber (Chicago: Aldine Publishing Co., 1965). A wealth of statistical data on Negro migration patterns and racial segregation in large urban areas is presented.

The Moynihan Report and the Politics of Controversy by Lee Rainwater and William L. Yancey (Cambridge, Mass.: M.I.T. Press, 1967). A discussion of the Moynihan controversy, including the debate over poverty versus cultural inheritance.

White Institutions
and Black Rage

DAVID BOESEL/RICHARD BERK/W. EUGENE GROVES

BETTYE EIDSON/PETER H. ROSSI

Five summers of black rebellion have made it clear that the United States is facing a crisis of proportions not seen since the Great Depression. And one of the root causes of this crisis, it has also become clear, is the performance of white institutions, especially those institutions in the ghetto. Some of these institutions—police and retail stores, for example —have done much to antagonize Negroes; others, such as welfare departments and black political organizations, have tried to help and have failed.

Why have these white institutions helped engender black rage? One way to find out might be to study the attitudes of the men working for them—to discover what their personnel think about the racial crisis itself, about their own responsibilities, about the work they are doing. Therefore, at the request of the National Advisory Commission on Civil Disorders (the riot commission), we at Johns Hopkins University visited 15 Northern cities and questioned men and women working for six different institutional groups: major employers, retail merchants, teachers, welfare workers, political workers (all Negro), and policemen. All of the people we questioned, except the employers, work right in the ghetto, and are rank-and-file employees—the cop on the beat, the social caseworker, and so on.

The "employers" we questioned were the managers or personnel officers of the ten institutions in each city that employed the most people, as well as an additional 20 managers or personnel officers of the next 100 institutions. As such, they represented the most economically progressive institutions in America. And in their employment policies we could see how some of America's dominant corporate institutions impinge on the everyday lives of urban Negroes.

Businessmen are in business to make a profit. Seldom do they run their enterprises for social objectives. But since it is fashionable these days, most of the managers and personnel officers we interviewed (86 percent, in fact) accepted the proposition that they "have a social responsibility to make strong efforts to provide employment for Negroes and other minority groups." This assertion, however, is contradicted by unemployment in the Negro community today, as well as by the hiring policies of the firms themselves.

Businessmen, as a whole, do not exhibit openly racist attitudes. Their position might best be described as one of "optimistic denial"—the gentlemanly white racism evident in a tacit, but often unwitting, acceptance of institutional practices that subordinate or exclude Negroes. One aspect of this optimistic denial is a nonrecognition of the seriousness of the problems that face black people. Only 21 percent of our sample thought that unemployment was a very serious problem in the nations' cities, yet 26 percent considered air pollution very serious and 31 percent considered traffic very serious. The employers' perspective is based upon their limited experience with blacks, and that experience does not give them a realistic picture of the plight of Negroes in this country. Employers don't even think that racial discrimination has much to do with the Negroes' plight; a majority (57 percent) felt that Negroes are treated at least as well as other people of the same income, and an additional 6 percent felt that Negroes are treated *better* than any other part of the population.

This optimistic denial on the part of employers ("things really aren't that bad for Negroes") is often combined with a negative image of Negroes as employees. Half of those employers interviewed (51 percent) said that Negroes are likely to have higher rates of absenteeism than whites, so that hiring many of them would probably upset production schedules. Almost a third thought that, because Negro crime rates are generally higher than white crime rates, hiring many Negroes could lead to increased theft and vandalism in their companies. About a fifth (22 percent) thought that hiring Negroes might bring "agitators and troublemakers" into their companies, and another one-fifth feared that production costs might rise because Negroes supposedly do not take orders well.

The employer's views may reflect not only traditional white prejudices, but also some occasional experience he himself has had with Negroes. Such experiences, however, may stem as much from the employer's own practices and misconceptions as from imputed cultural habits of Negroes. As Elliott Liebow observed in his study of Negro street-corner men *(Talley's Corner)*, blacks have learned to cope with life by treating menial, low-status, degrading jobs in the same way that the jobs treat them—with benign nonconcern.

Most of the employers believe that Negroes lack the preparation for anything but menial jobs. A full 83 percent said that few Negroes are qualified for professional jobs, and 69 percent thought that few are qualified for skilled positions. When it comes to unskilled jobs, of course, only 23 percent of the employers held this view. The employers seem to share a widespread assumption— one frequently used as a cover for racism—that for historical and environmental reasons Negroes have been disabled to such an extent as to make them uncompetitive in a highly competitive society. And while it is certainly true that black people have suffered from a lack of educational and other opportunities, this line of thinking—especially among whites—has a tendency to blame the past and the ghetto environment for what is perceived as Negro incompetence, thus diverting attention from *present* institutional practices. So, many employers have developed a rhetoric of concern about upgrading the so-called "hardcore unemployed" in lieu of changing their employment policies.

To a considerable extent our respondents' assessment of Negro job qualifications reflects company policy, for the criteria used in hiring skilled and professional workers tend to exclude Negroes. The criteria are (1) previous experience and (2) recommendations. It is evident that because Negroes are unlikely to have *had* previous experience in positions from which they have long been excluded, and because they are unlikely to have had much contact with people in the best position to recommend them, the criteria for "qualification" make it probable that employers will consider most Negroes unqualified.

In short, the employers' aversion to taking risks (at least with people), reinforced by the pressure of labor unions and more general discriminatory patterns in society, means that Negroes usually get the worst jobs.

Thus, although Negroes make up 20 percent of the unskilled workers in these large corporations, they fill only a median of one percent of the professional positions and only 2 percent of the skilled positions. Moreover, the few Negroes in the higher positions are unevenly distributed among the corporations. Thirty-two percent of the companies don't report Negroes in professional positions, and 24 percent do not report any in skilled positions. If these companies are set aside, in the remaining companies the median percentage of Negroes in the two positions rises to 3 percent and 6 percent respectively. Further, in these remaining companies an even larger percentage (8 percent in both cases) of *current* positions are being filled by Negroes—which indicates, among other things, that a breakthrough has been accomplished in some companies, while in others Negro employment in the upper levels remains minimal or nonexistent.

Even among those companies that hire blacks for skilled jobs, a Negro applicant's chances of getting the job are only one-fourth as good as those of his white counterpart. For professional positions, the chances are more nearly equal: Negro applicants are about three-fourths as likely to get these jobs as are white applicants. It seems that Negroes have come closest to breaking in at the top (though across all firms only about 4 percent of the applicants for professional positions are Negro). The real stumbling-block to equal employment opportunities seems to be at the skilled level, and here it may be that union policies—and especially those of the craft unions—augment the employers' resistance to hiring Negroes for and promoting Negroes to skilled positions.

What do urban Negroes themselves think of employers' hiring practices? A survey of the same 15 cities by Angus Campbell and Howard Schuman, for the riot commission, indicates that one-third (34 percent) of the Negro men interviewed reported having been refused jobs because of racial discrimination, and 72 percent believed that some or many other black applicants are turned down for the same reason. Almost as many (68 percent) think that some or many black people miss out on promotions because of prejudice. And even when companies do hire Negroes (presumably in professional positions), this is interpreted as tokenism: 7.7 percent of the black respondents thought that Negroes are hired by big companies for show purposes.

The companies we studied, which have little contact with

the ghetto, are very different from the other institutions in our survey, whose contact with the ghetto is direct and immediate. The corporations are also up-to-date, well-financed, and innovative, while the white institutions inside the ghetto are outdated, underfinanced, and overloaded. In historical terms, the institutions in the ghetto represent another era of thought and organization.

The slum merchants illustrate the tendency of ghetto institutions to hark back to earlier forms. While large corporations cooperate with one another and with the government to exert substantial control over their market, the ghetto merchant still functions in the realm of traditional laissez-faire. He is likely to be a small operator, economically marginal and with almost no ability to control his market. His main advantage over the more efficient, modern retailer is his restricted competition, for the ghetto provides a captive market. The difficulty that many blacks have in getting transportation out of the ghetto, combined with a lack of experience in comparative shopping, seems to give the local merchant a competitive aid he sorely needs to survive against the lower prices and better goods sold in other areas of the city.

The merchants in our study also illustrate the free-enterprise character of ghetto merchandising. They run very small operations—grocery stores, restaurants, clothing and liquor stores, and so on, averaging a little over three employees per business. Almost half of them (45 percent) find it difficult to "keep up with their competition" (competition mainly *within* the ghetto). Since there are almost no requirements for becoming a merchant, this group is the most heterogeneous of all those studied. They have the widest age range (from 17 through 80), the highest percentage of immigrants (15 percent), and the lowest educational levels (only 16 percent finished college).

Again in contrast to the large corporations, the ghetto merchant must live with the harsh day-to-day realities of violence and poverty. His attitudes toward Negroes, different in degree from those of the employers, are at least partly a function of his objective evaluations of his customers.

Running a business in a ghetto means facing special kinds of "overhead." Theft is an especially worrisome problem for the merchants; respondents mentioned it more frequently than any other problem. There is, of course, some basis in fact for their concern. According to the riot commission, inventory losses—ordinarily under 2 percent of sales—may be twice as great in high-crime areas (most of which are in ghettos). And for these small businesses such losses may cut substantially into a slender margin of profit.

Thus it is not surprising that, of all the occupational groups interviewed in this study, the retail merchants were among the most likely to consider Negroes violent and criminal. For example, 61 percent said that Negroes are more likely to steal than whites, and 50 percent believed that Negroes are more likely to pass bad checks. No wonder, then, that black customers may encounter unusual surveillance and suspicion when they shop.

Less understandable is the ghetto merchant's apparent ignorance of the plight of ghetto blacks. Thus, 75 percent believe that blacks get medical treatment that is equal to or better than what whites get. A majority think that Negroes are not discriminated against with regard to treatment by the police, recreation facilities and so forth. Logically enough, 51 percent of the merchants feel that Negroes are making too many demands. This percentage is the second-highest measured (the police were the least sympathetic). So the merchants (like all other groups in the survey except the black politicians) are inclined to emphasize perceived defects in the black community as a major problem in their dealings with Negroes.

The shaky economic position of the merchants, their suspicion of their Negro customers, and the high "overhead" of doing business in the ghetto (because of theft, vandalism, bad credit risks) lead many merchants to sell inferior merchandise at higher prices—and to resort to other stratagems for getting money out of their customers. To elicit responses from the merchants on such delicate matters, we drew up a series of very indirect questions. The responses we obtained, though they no doubt understate the extent to which ghetto merchants provide a poor dollar value per unit of goods, are nevertheless revealing. For example, we asked the merchants to recommend various ways of "keeping up with business competition." Some 44 percent said that you should offer extra services; over a third (36 percent) said you should raise prices to cover unusually high overhead; and the same number (36 percent) said that you should buy "bargain" goods at lower prices, then sell them at regular prices. (To a small merchant, "bargain goods" ordinarily means "seconds," or slightly spoiled merchandise, because he doesn't do enough volume to gain real discounts from a wholesaler.) A smaller but still significant segment (12 percent) said that one should "bargain the selling price with each customer and take whatever breaks you can get."

The Campbell-Schuman study indicates that 56 percent of the Negroes interviewed felt that they had been overcharged in neighborhood stores (24 percent said often); 42 percent felt that they had been sold spoiled or inferior goods (13 percent said often). Given the number of ghetto stores a customer may visit every week, these data are entirely compatible with ours. Since one-third of the merchants indicated that they were not averse to buying "bargain" goods for sale in their stores, it is understandable that 42 percent of the Negroes in these areas should say that at one time or another they have been sold inferior merchandise.

It is also understandable that during the recent civil disorders many Negroes, unable to affect merchants by routine methods, struck directly at the stores, looting and burning them.

Just as ghetto merchants are in a backwater of the economy, ghetto schools are in a backwater of the educational system, experimental efforts in some cities notwithstanding.

Negroes, of course, are most likely to be served by outmoded and inadequate schools, a fact that the Coleman Report has documented in considerable detail. In metropolitan regions of the Northeast, for example, 40 percent of the Negro pupils at the secondary level attended schools in buildings over 40 years old, but only 15 percent of the whites did; the average number of pupils per room was 35 for Negroes but 28 for whites.

The teachers covered in our survey (half of whom were Negro) taught in ghetto schools at all levels. Surprisingly, 88 percent said that they were satisfied with their jobs. Their rate of leaving, however, was not consistent with this. Half of the teachers had been in their present schools for no more than four years. Breaking the figures down year by year, we find that the largest percentage (17 percent) had been there only one year. In addition, the teachers' rate of leaving increased dramatically after they had taught for five years.

While the teachers thought that education was a major problem for the cities and especially for the ghettos, they did not think that ghetto schools were a source of the difficulty. A solid majority, comparing their own schools with others in the city, thought that theirs were average, above average, or superior in seven out of eight categories. The high quality of the teaching staff, so rated by 84 percent of the respondents, was rivaled only by the high quality of the textbooks (again 84 percent). The one doubtful area, according to the teachers, was the physical plant, which seemed to them to be just barely competitive; in this respect, 44 percent considered their own schools below average or inferior.

The teachers have less confidence in their students than in themselves or their schools. On the one hand, they strongly reject the view that in ghetto schools education is sacrificed to the sheer need for order: 85 percent said it was not true that pupils in their schools were uneducable, and that teachers could do little more than maintain discipline. On the other hand, the teachers as a group could not agree that their students were as educable as they might be. There was little consensus on whether their pupils were "about average" in interest and ability: 28 percent thought that their pupils were; 41 percent thought it was partially true that they were; and 31 percent thought it was not true. But the teachers had less difficulty agreeing that their students were *not* "above average in ability and . . . generally co-operative with teachers." Agreeing on this were 59 percent of the teachers, with another 33 percent in the middle.

The real problem with education in the ghetto, as the teachers see it, is the ghetto itself. The teachers have their own version of the "Negro disability" thesis: the "cultural deprivation" theory holds that the reason for bad education in the ghetto is the student's environment rather than the schools. (See "How Teachers Learn to Help Children Fail," by Estelle Fuchs, September, 1968.) Asked to name the major problems facing their schools, the teachers most frequently mentioned community apathy; the second most-mentioned problem, a derivation of the first, was an alleged lack of preparation and motivation in the students. Fifty-nine percent of the teachers agreed to some extent that "many communities provide such a terrible environment for the pupils that education doesn't do much good in the end."

Such views are no doubt detrimental to education in the ghetto, for they imply a decided fatalism as far as teaching is concerned. If the students are deficient—improperly motivated, distracted, and so on—and if the cause of this deficiency lies in the ghetto rather than in the schools themselves, then there is little reason for a teacher to exert herself to set high standards for her students.

There is considerable question, however, whether the students in ghetto schools are as distracted as the teachers think. Events in the last few years indicate that the schools, especially the high schools and the junior high schools, are one of the strongest focuses of the current black rebellion. The student strike at Detroit's Northern High School in 1966, for example, was cohesive and well-organized. A boycott by some 2,300 students, directed against a repressive school administration, lasted over two weeks and resulted in the dismissal of the principal and the formation of a committee, including students, to investigate school conditions. The ferment in the ghetto schools across the country is also leading to the formation of permanent and independent black students' groups, such as the Modern Strivers in Washington, D.C.'s Eastern High, intent on promoting black solidarity and bringing about changes in the educational system. In light of such developments, there is reason to think that the teachers in the survey have· overestimated the corrosive effects of the ghetto environment on students—and underestimated the schools' responsibility for the state of education in the ghetto.

Public welfare is another area in which old ideas have been perpetuated beyond their time. The roots of the present welfare-department structure lie in the New Deal legislation of the 1930s. The public assistance provisions of the Social Security Act were designed to give aid to the helpless and the noncompetitive: the aged, the blind, the "permanently and totally" disabled, and dependent children. The assumption was that the recipient, because of personal disabilities or inadequacies, could not make his way in life without outside help.

The New Deal also provided work (e.g., the W.P.A.) for the able-bodied who were assumed to be unemployed only temporarily. But as the Depression gave way to the war years and to the return of prosperity, the massive work programs for the able-bodied poor were discontinued, leaving only those programs that were premised on the notion of personal disability. To a considerable extent today's Negro poor have had to rely on the latter. Chief among these programs, of course, is Aid for Dependent Children, which has become a mainstay of welfare. And because of racial discrimination, especially in education and employment, a large part of the Negro population also experiences poverty as a permanent state.

While most of the social workers in our survey showed considerable sympathy with the Negro cause, they too felt that the root of the problem lay in weaknesses in the Negro community; and they saw their primary task as making up the supposed deficiency. A hefty majority of the respondents (78 percent) thought that a large part of their responsibility was to "teach the poor how to live"—rather than to provide the means for them to live as they like. Assuming disability, welfare has fostered dependency.

The social workers, however, are unique among the groups surveyed in that they are quite critical of their own institution. The average welfare worker is not entirely at one with the establishment for which she works. She is likely to be a college graduate who regards her job as transitional. And her lack of expertise has its advantages as well as its disadvantages, for it means that she can take a more straightforward view of the situations she is confronted with. She is not committed to bureaucracy as a way of life.

The disparity between the welfare establishment and the average welfare worker is evident in the latter's complaints about her job. The complaints she voices the most deal *not* with her clients, but with the welfare department itself and the problems of working within its present structure—the difficulty of getting things done, the red tape, the lack of adequate funds, and so on. Of the five most-mentioned difficulties of welfare work, three dealt with such intra-agency problems; the other two dealt with the living conditions of the poor.

There is a good deal of evidence to support the social worker's complaints. She complains, for example, that welfare agencies are understaffed. The survey indicates that an average caseload is 177 people, each client being visited about once a month for about 50 minutes. Even the most conscientious of caseworkers must be overwhelmed by such client-to-worker ratios.

As in the case of the schools, welfare has engendered a countervailing force among the very people it is supposed to serve. Welfare clients have become increasingly hostile to the traditional structure and philosophy of welfare departments and have formed themselves into an outspoken movement. The welfare-rights movement at this stage has aims: to obtain a more nearly adequate living base for the clients, and to overload the system with demands, thus either forcing significant changes or clearing the way for new and more appropriate institutions.

Usually when segments of major social institutions become incapable of functioning adequately, the people whom the institutions are supposed to serve have recourse to politics. In the ghetto, however, the political machinery is no better off than the other institutions. Around the turn of the century Negroes began to carve out small niches for themselves in the politics of such cities as Chicago and New York. Had Negro political organizations developed along the same lines as those of white ethnic groups, they might today provide valuable leverage for the ghetto population. But this has not happened. For one thing, the decline of the big-city machine, and its replacement in many cities by "nonpolitical" reform governments supported by a growing middle class, began to close off a route traditionally open to minority groups. Second, black politicians have never been regarded as fullfledged political brokers by racist whites, and consequently the possibility of a Negro's becoming a powerful politician in a predominantly white city has been foreclosed (the recent election of Carl Stokes as

Mayor of Cleveland and Richard D. Hatcher, Mayor of Gary, Indiana, would be exceptions). Whites have tended to put aside their differences when confronting Negro political efforts; to regard Negro demands, no matter how routine, as racial issues; and hence to severely limit the concessions made to black people.

Today the sphere of Negro politics is cramped and closely circumscribed. As Kenneth B. Clark has observed, most of the Negroes who have reached high public office have done so *not* within the context of Negro politics, but through competition in the larger society. In most cities Negro political organizations are outmoded and inadequate. Even if, as seems probable, more and more Negro mayors are elected, they will have to work within the antiquated structure of urban government, with sharply limited resources. Unless things change, the first Negro mayor of Newark, for example, will preside over a bankrupt city.

Our survey of Negro political workers in the 15 cities documents the inadequacy of Negro politics—and the inadequacy of the larger system of urban politics. The political workers, understandably, strongly sympathize with the aspirations of other black people. As ghetto politicians, they deal with the demands and frustrations of other blacks day after day. Of all the groups surveyed, they were the most closely in touch with life in the ghetto. Most of them work in the middle and lower levels of municipal politics; they talk with about 75 voters each week. These political workers are, of course, acutely aware of the precipitous rise in the demands made by the black community. Most (93 percent) agreed that in the last few years people in their districts have become more determined to get what they want. The stongest impetus of this new determination comes from the younger blacks: 92 percent of the political workers agreed that "young people have become more militant." Only a slight majority, however (56 percent), said the same of middle-aged people.

Against the pressure of rising Negro demands, urban po-

litical organizations formed in other times and on other assumptions, attentive to other interests, and constrained by
severely limited resources, find themselves unable to respond satisfactorily. A majority of the political workers, in
evaluating a variety of services available to people in their
districts, thought that all except two—telephone service
and the fire department—were either poor or fair. Worst
of the lot, according to the political workers, were recreation, police protection, and building inspection.

In view of these respondents, the black community has
no illusions about the ability of routine politics to meet its
needs. While only 38 percent of the political workers
thought that the people in their districts regarded their
councilmen as friends fighting for them, 51 percent said
that the people considered their councilmen "part of the
city government which must be asked continually and repeatedly in order to get things done." (Since the political
workers were probably talking about their fellow party
members, their responses may have been more favorable
than frank. A relatively high percentage of "don't know"
responses supports this point.)

Almost all the Negro politicians said that they received
various requests from the voters for help. Asked whether
they could respond to these requests "almost always, usually, or just sometimes," the largest percentage (36 percent)
chose "sometimes"—which, in context, is a way of saying
"seldom." Another 31 percent said they "usually" could
respond to such requests, and 19 percent said "almost always." Logically enough, 60 percent of the political workers
agreed that in the last few years "people have become more
fed up with the system, and are becoming unwilling to
work with politicians." In effect, this is an admission that
they as political workers, and the system of urban politics
to which they devote themselves, are failing.

When economic and social institutions fail to provide
the life-chances that a substantial part of a population
wants, and when political institutions fail to provide a rem-

edy, the aspirations of the people begin to spill over into forms of activity that the dominant society regards either as unacceptable or illegitimate—crime, vandalism, noncooperation, and various forms of political protest.

Robert M. Fogelson and Robert D. Hill, in the *Supplemental Studies* for the riot commission, have reported that 50 percent to 90 percent of the Negro males in ten cities studied had arrest records. Clearly, when the majority of men in a given population are defined as criminals—at least by the police—something more than "deviant" behaviour is involved. In effect, ghetto residents—and especially the youth—and the police are in a state of subdued warfare. On the one hand, the cities are experiencing a massive and as yet inchoate social rising of the Negro population. On the other hand, the police—devoted to the racial status quo and inclined to overlook the niceties of mere law in their quest for law and order—have found a variety of means, both conventional and otherwise, for countering the aims of Negroes. In doing so, they are not only adhering to the norms of their institution, but also furthering their personal goals as well. The average policeman, recruited from a lower- or middle-class white background, frequently of "ethnic" origins, comes from a group whose social position is marginal and who feel most threatened by Negro advances.

The high arrest rate in the Negro community thus mirrors both the push of Negroes and the determined resistance of the police. As the conflict intensifies, the police are more and more losing authority in the eyes of black people; the young Negroes are especially defiant. Any type of contact between police and black people can quickly lead to a situation in which the policeman gives an order and the Negro either defies it or fails to show sufficient respect in obeying it. This in turn can lead to the Negro's arrest on a disorderly conduct charge or on a variety of other charges. (Disorderly conduct accounted for about 17 percent of the arrests in the Fogelson-Hill study.)

The police often resort to harassment as a means of keeping the Negro community off-balance. The riot commission noted that:

Because youths commit a large and increasing proportion of crime, police are under growing pressure from their supervisors—and from the community—to deal with them forcefully. "Harassment of youths" may therefore be viewed by some police departments—and members even of the Negro community—as a proper crime prevention technique.

The Commission added that "many departments have adopted patrol practices which, in the words of one commentator, have 'replaced harassment by individual patrolmen with harassment by entire departments.'"

Among the most common of the cops' harassment techniques are breaking up street-corner groups and stop-and-frisk tactics. Our study found that 63 percent of the ghetto police reported that they "frequently" were called upon to disperse loitering groups. About a third say they "frequently" stop and frisk people. Obviously then, the law enforcer sometimes interferes with individuals and groups who consider their activities quite legitimate and necessary. Black people in the ghetto—in the absence of adequate parks, playgrounds, jobs, and recreation facilities, and unwilling to sit in sweltering and overcrowded houses with rats and bugs—are likely to make the streets their front yards. But this territory is often made uninhabitable by the police.

Nearly a third of the white policemen in our study thought that most of the residents of their precinct (largely Negro) were not industrious. Even more striking about the attitudes of the white police working in these neighborhoods is that many of them deny the fact of Negro inequality: 20 percent say the Negro is treated better than any other part of the population, and 14 percent say he is treated equally. As for their own treatment of Negroes, the Campbell-Schuman survey reported that 43 percent of the black men, who are on the streets more than the women, thought that police use insulting language in their neighborhoods. Only 17 percent of the white males held this belief. Of the Negro men, 20 percent reported that the police insulted them personally and 28 percent said they knew someone to whom this had happened; only 9 percent and 12 percent, respectively, of the whites reported the same. Similarly, many more blacks than whites thought that the police frisked and searched people without good reason (42 percent compared to 12 percent) ; and that the police roughed up people unnecessarily (37 percent as compared to 10 percent). Such reports of police misconduct were most frequent among the younger Negroes, who, after all, are on the receiving end most often.

The policeman's isolation in the ghetto is evident in a number of findings. We asked the police how many people —of various types—they knew well enough in the ghetto to greet when they saw them. Eighty-nine percent of the police said they knew six or more shopowners, managers, and clerks well enough to speak with, but only 38 percent said they knew this many teenage or youth leaders. At the same time, 39 percent said that most young adults, and 51 percent said that most adolescents, regard the police as enemies. And only 16 percent of the white policemen (37 percent of the blacks) either "often" or "sometimes" attended meetings in the neighborhood.

The police have wound up face to face with the social consequences of the problems in the ghetto created by the failure of other white institutions—though, as has been observed, they themselves have contributed to those problems in no small degree. The distant and gentlemanly white racism of employers, the discrimination of white parents who object to having their children go to school with Negroes, the disgruntlement of white taxpayers who deride the present welfare system as a sinkhole of public funds but are unwilling to see it replaced by anything more effective—the consequences of these and other forms of white racism have confronted the police with a massive control problem of the kind most evident in the riots.

In our survey, we found that the police were inclined to see the riots as the long range result of faults in the Negro community—disrespect for law, crime, broken families, etc.—rather than as responses to the stance of the white community. Indeed, nearly one-third of the white police saw the riots as the result of what they considered the basic violence and disrespect of Negroes in general, while only one-fourth attributed the riots to the failure of white institutions. More than three-fourths also regarded the riots as the immediate result of agitators and criminals—a suggestion contradicted by all the evidence accumulated by the riot commission. The police, then, share with the other groups—excepting the black politicians—a tendency to emphasize perceived defects in the black community as an explanation for the difficulties that they encounter in the ghetto.

The state of siege evident in many police departments is but an exaggerated version of a trend in the larger white society. It is the understandable, but unfortunate, response of people who are angry and confused about the widespread disruption of traditional racial patterns and who feel threatened by these changes. There is, of course, some basis for this feeling, because the Negro movement poses challenges of power and interest to many groups. To the extent that the movement is successful, the merchants, for example, will either have to reform their practices or go out of business—and for many it may be too late for reform. White suburbanites will have to cough up funds for the city, which provides most of them with employment. Police departments will have to be thoroughly restructured.

The broad social rising of Negroes is beginning to have a substantial effect upon all white institutions in the ghetto, as the situation of the merchants, the schools, and the welfare establishment illustrates. Ten years ago, these institutions (and the police, who have been affected differently) could operate pretty much unchecked by any countervailing power in the ghetto. Today, both their excesses and their inadequacies have run up against an increasingly militant black population, many of whom support violence as a means of redress. The evidence suggests that unless these institutions are transformed, the black community will make it increasingly difficult for them to function at all.

March 1969

Breakdown in Law and Order

TOM PARMENTER

Spokesmen and public men, preachers and newspaper columnists need only open their mouths in the face of a Detroit or a Newark or a Watts and the phrase "breakdown of law and order" comes rolling out. The cliche has much to commend it to such men. Certainly neither "They're breeding like hamsters down there" or "We need to set up a pilot program" quite covers the situation and until the time comes to say "We must appoint a committee" nothing is quite so appropriate as "breakdown."

Cliches are convenient. No one in love or in mourning uses anything else. And as shorthand expressions of public figures they make the work of a reporter lighter. The danger comes when the cliche becomes reality, when it turns into an explanation. In the case of Detroit and the other urban riots, "breakdown of law and order" means looting and snipers, soup lines, broken windows and broken lives, corpses and sirens, and calling out the troops. This is the meaning of the phrase to the public men who use it, but the phrase may have another meaning to the Negroes of Detroit.

I spent several days in Detroit as the riots were running down gathering material on encounters ·with the police. What appears below is not the truth that may eventually emerge from trials, grand-jury investigations, and committees, but the truth as perceived by those involved in the events.

The Detroit riots started in a police raid on what is known locally with self-conscious quaintness as a blind pig, an after-hours tavern. The police began to move the eighty patrons to the precinct station for booking and downtown to jail. The police guard around the building attracted a crowd even at 5 a.m. Someone smashed the window of a squad car. Within minutes the crowd began to move down 12th Street breaking windows and looting. A shoe store was torched and the crowd grew. One of the first official acts of the police commissioner was to block off Belle Isle Park, the island which saw the worst of the 1943 riot. Despite the trouble, the night police watch went off duty as usual at 8 a.m. and the day watch came on. At the same time, things began to quiet down a bit. The crowd milled around the streets, good-tempered if sarcastic. The police increased their guard.

"They were intimidating the hell out of the streets, man," said a Negro community organizer who was on 12th Street that Sunday morning. "It was the most insane thing you'd want to see. They just occupied 12th Street. Ninety God-damn degrees, Sunday morning, and they just occupy that street. They thought about pulling off but they waited until too late. The tension was bad, man. And the police recognized it and said, 'Well, maybe we'd better get out of here a little bit,' you know? Between 9 a.m. and the time they pulled some of the police out, that's when it really got going. Cats was walking up and down the streets drinking blood and saying 'We're going to burn it. We're going to smoke it up and we don't want nobody down there talking no shit.' "

"It was just too late. It would have erupted sooner or later. There was nothing to do *then*. I mean it was all over. What they should have done when they busted that blind pig and these cats broke in those three stores, they should have boarded those stores up and got the hell out of there and then sent some detectives in there or something. But these cats boarded the damned things up and blocked off 12th Street and when people came out in the morning here they are with shotguns on the God-damned streets. If that's not the most stupid thing. They just made mistake after mistake. And they miscalculated in so God-damn many areas. I mean it can only go so long. I mean the probability of this kind of thing happening under the *law enforcement* process here in Detroit. It was time for something to happen. These cats have gotten away with so much shit, man. They ran down Negroes on *horses* in Belle Isle last year, man. There was no riot until these cats started it. They tried to start the riot four days earlier down on Butternut."

The incident referred to took place about three miles from the blind pig. A disturbance had started over a disorderly conduct arrest. "They called in the rest of the dogs down there, man. In four minutes, it was 20 squad cars in that block. Police was all over the place, you know. And there they was with these shotguns, all prepared with riot tactics. It was an integrated crowd standing around watching, you know. It was irresponsibility. Four days later they did the same damned thing on 12th Street but they was in the wrong part of town. It blew up.

"The *whole thing* was showing force. That's all they was doing was showing force, intimidating purposely. The policy of showing force went straight on to the other end, man. Three hours after these cats were showing force with the Detroit police department down here on 12th Street, the law had broke down completely."

The riot started again in full force about noon on Sunday. A young man described for me his usual way of life and his part in the riots. Call him Arthur.

"I'm making more money than the average white man with a white collar job," he said.

"How is that?"

"Well, I make mine."

"Hustling?"

"Well," he smiled and went on, "I do a little bit of everything. I don't steal for it. I don't rob nobody. I mean I can't go to jail unless somebody tell on me, you understand? And I don't think they're going to tell on me because they love me."

"How did you hear about the riot?"

"I heard a friend of mine say, 'Hey! They rioting up on 12th.' I said what are they doing and he said *looting.* That's all it *took* to get me *out* of the house. He said the police was letting them take it; they wasn't stopping it; so I said it was time for me to get some of these diamonds and watches and rings. It wasn't that I was mad at anybody or angry or trying to get back at the white man. If I saw something that I could get without getting hurt, I got it."

Arthur's assertion that he wasn't trying to get back at anyone was not assured. He did agree that he was stealing.

"This is nothing but pure lawlessness. People are trying to get what they can get. They *have* been *denied* these things and when the first brick was thrown, that's all it took. Let's get it while we can get it. They were trying to get all they could get. They got diamonds here, they got money here, they got clothes here and TV's and what not. What could they do with it when they bring it out except sell it to each other? That's all. They're just getting something they haven't got. I mean, I bought me some clothes from somebody. I have exchanged whiskey and different things for different things. You know, something I wanted that I didn't have. This was a good way to get it. *I really enjoyed myself.*

"I didn't get caught until Sunday night. I got caught because I was going into one of them little bitty stores instead of going in one of them big stores. I went to a stocking store because I was going to get my girl friend some stockings. I had three or four hundred pair under my arm when I come out. They told me to put 'em down.

"Before that the police weren't stopping me. What have we got them for? They *could* have stopped it. I'd come up and I'd have an armful of clothes or a bagful of diamonds and he'd say, 'Having fun?' I'd say 'Plenty of it.' I'd take them on and go back and get some more. If he had pulled a gun and said drop it it would have been dropped. I wouldn't have picked up nothing else. But they seemed to be enjoying seeing 12th Street tore down."

"Why?"

"For the prostitutes. That's the *only* reason. It's more prostitutes than it is people living there.

"I thought it was a lot of fun. People see'n what they could get for nothing and they went out and got it. It wasn't no race riot. They was white and Negro both going in stores and helping each other pass things out. Having a good time. Really enjoying themselves until them *fools* [snipers] started shooting. I hope they can get them because they're stopping me from making my money.

"Before that you didn't even have to go in a store to get nothing. All you had to do was tell people you saw with a bunch of stuff, 'Hey buddy, let me get some of that.' They'd give you some. One guy had ten suits and I had two; he gave me three. That's the way it was. It wasn't no organized stuff. Everybody was trying to get in it. I went in one place there was about 10 hands in a safe trying to get the money. Like I said, I really enjoyed myself.

"The only thing was that we had a minority group that was going around burning. I really do believe it was organized. They waited until stuff got going. See? What they tried to do was shoot off a few police officers and see if everybody would get armed. That's ridiculous."

The snipers in Detroit 1967—there were snipers there in 1943 as well—attracted a great deal of attention, and not only from adherents of devil theories. It is widely believed by Detroit officials that fewer than a dozen snipers —white and Negro—ever fired a gun in Detroit during the riots. Although police reports make frequent mention of sniper fire in the area of a number of the riot deaths, even the daily tally issued during the riots by police attributed only two deaths to sniper fire. In comparison, 22 deaths were attributed to shootings by police, soldiers, private guards, and store owners. Of these, 14 were killed by the Detroit police. All the deaths occurred after the first day of looting described above.

Three of the deaths for which the police nominated snipers as a probable source may become a greater cause celebre than the riots themselves. Three days after I gathered most of the following material, the deaths hit the front pages of the Detroit papers. The implication was police execution. Since then, several investigations of the incident have been announced.

The first police reports implied that three youths had been killed in an exchange of gunfire between police and snipers in an annex to the Algiers Motel. (The annex is located on a pleasant tree-lined street not at all untypical of Detroit's Negro neighborhoods.) No guns were found in the rooms where the bodies were found, however, and the police were informed of the deaths anonymously—not by an official source.

One witness was Michael Clark, 19. His roommate, Carl Cooper, 17, was killed. "There was no shooting around the motel at all. We was just sitting in the room doing nothing. The first shooting I knew about came from the cops. I looked out and there was a state trooper pointing a rifle up into the window. Carl ran down the hall. I guess they shot him downstairs. That's where the body was. He was dead when we got down. They said they was going to shoot us one at a time. Called us niggers. I heard them shoot Fred Temple after they took him out. They just kept on beating us and beating us all the time. Then they told me to come into a room and they pointed a gun in my face. Told me to lay down and then he shot. He shot above me. I don't know why he didn't shoot me. Then I heard another shot across the hall. I guess that was Aubrey Pollard when they shot him. I don't know why they did it. I got out of there. But I'm going to testify. I've already talked to the detectives."

Cooper's funeral was a Jessica Mitford affair held in a funeral home so "tasteful" that it looked like an architect's drawing rather than a building in use. Clark was one of the pallbearers. "I knew Carl since we was little kids."

Cooper's family and friends seemed the sort known as "the good people of the Negro community." They were decorous people, well-dressed and driving good cars. They were not necessarily middle class, but they were urban people, not poverty-stricken Southern migrants dressed uncomfortably in their mail-order suits and Sunday dresses. The body was lying in an open coffin. The minister offered his comforting best to a background of weeping. After everyone had passed the body, curtains were drawn across the front of the room, hiding the pulpit and the body. Suddenly, the room erupted in a surge of emotion. Women screamed and several charged the curtain only to be led away by attendants. The family seating section lost all semblance of regularity as women began to rock back and forth and soon everyone was moving around the room. The funeral director eyed his watch; another cortege was waiting to move into the chapel. The women who had been led away went back into the room. The minister offered more words and then the curtains were reopened and Clark and the other pallbearers moved the coffin out to the hearse.

The stories about investigations of the death were not yet public, but they were common knowledge among the several hundred gathered for Cooper's funeral. In fact, the stories were being heard all over the West side soon after the deaths early Wednesday. Arthur, the hustler quoted above, hangs around the Algiers and although he was unwilling to admit it to himself, it was only happenstance that he was not killed himself.

Arthur wasn't at Cooper's funeral, although he said he was closer to him than to the other two who were killed. His ambivalence about race is apparent as he talks about politics and grief. "I think Johnson is for the Negroes. He has to be to be President. I would be for anybody in the world if they was going to elect me President. Everybody's talking about Abe Lincoln freeing the slaves but there was only one man who was really for the Negroes and that was Kennedy. You see what they did to him. That's the only man—white man, black man, green man—that I ever cried for when he got killed. That was the man."

"Did you cry over these kids?"

"Naw. I didn't cry over them. I mean, that's life. They wasn't doing anything for me. Kennedy was trying to help me. I felt bad about them, but the first thing that hit my mind was, 'I'm glad it wasn't me.' That's the only thing I thought about."

His first words when asked about the shootings were, "It was murder. They just murdered them boys. They just happened to be with these white girls, all of them sitting up in the room together. That's what it was. We was standing outside and the guard here at the motel said it's curfew time and we had to get in. So they went around with them and we went on in our place. That's the deal.

"There were plenty of cops around. When we opened the door to see—we heard some shooting—just a crack more or less and a shotgun or a rifle came into the door and told us to come on out of there. That's what we did. I didn't know who it was and I didn't care. I was coming out even if it had been a sniper, but I was coming out.

"When the other bunch come downstairs one of them was in the hall already dead. That's Carl. I know for a fact that Carl was not the kind of guy to be raising no whole lot of hell. If a policeman put a drop on him he's going to raise them up like he's supposed to. He was dead. They killed him. Then they shot the other two and then just called downtown and said it's three bodies up in back of the Algiers. They didn't do no reporting other than that, no numbers or saying they was policemen or nothing.

"There wasn't any rioting or anything closer than six

blocks away. I did hear about some blank pistol or something being shot but that wasn't close." [Newspaper reports stated that Cooper had a starter's pistol, but none was found.]

Arthur continued: "I think it must be because the white girls was in the room with them. I really do. It was just cold-blooded murder. They asked the girls, 'Which one of you white whores is fucking one of these black niggers?' Before the girl could say something he hit her in the head. He beat her down. They hit her in the head with the rifle."

A second young man—he gave his name as Boston Blackie and said he was a pimp—broke into the conversation. "I'm going to tell you what the whole deal was. They probably didn't know how it happened, seeing these white girls in this room with these Negroes. They didn't give nobody a chance to explain themselves. All cops are probably prejudiced to an extent. This girl that was hit told me the officer was in the late thirties or early forties. She said he seemed like he was nuts. She said he came in talking that shit about a white woman in there. At first I didn't believe it when I heard it. Then I was sick when I came over and found out. They said this one guy who was giving the orders seemed like he was mentally unbalanced or something. The dude *had* to be crazy. He was talking about who wants to die first the girls or the fellows. She thought he was going to shoot her, too, after he hit her on the head."

Arthur continued: "They had us all out there in the court by the swimming pool. They didn't tell us to lay down or nothing. I asked *them* if there was going to *be* any shooting to let me lay down. I didn't want to be standing up because they had jeeps out here with these 50 calibers pointed this way and I didn't want them to shoot me. I was already scared of being shot at. It was a half hour after they laid us down that we found out that the boys was dead. One of the security guards around the motel walked one of the girls back to her room and when they walked in the hallway the boys was in there dead. The police had gone.

"They left the bodies here. You wouldn't expect them to stay after committing murder. The boys was laying down when they shot them. They looked for bullet holes and couldn't find them till they looked on the floor.

"I really thought Michael was dead. That's what they told me. I really thought he was dead until he showed up today. He came in here and said, 'Well, I'm not dead, y'all.'

"Now why did all this happen? What kind of shit is this? They don't turn in no report on who they are or nothing. That's nothing but murder. That's all it was and all it could be.

"If the boys *was* up there shooting *out* the window, *get on up there* and shoot *in* the window. Don't be just shooting all over the place. They could kill anybody. They had the boys in there and they had them up against the wall. They could have called the paddy wagon or whatever they wanted and took them downtown. They didn't have to kill the boys. They had no business over there. They wasn't doing shit in that room. They wasn't even playing cards like we was. They said they heard some shots and that's all it took. If I had had a cap pistol they'd be liable to come in there shooting instead of saying 'what is it' or 'come on out.' They just went in shooting."

"They just went in shooting." The words were repeated to describe one of the last deaths in the riot. The following material was gathered less than an hour after the death, at the same time that the street was hearing it first.

An inquest or trial may turn up a different and perhaps more correct story, but a story that will be heard by dozens as compared to the far greater number who heard the story as it appears here.

Of all those killed in the riots in Detroit, regular army paratroopers killed one, this one. The national guardsmen killed three, according to a police summary. Policemen are accustomed to working alone or with a partner. The closest they get to tactics—and it happens rarely in the normal course of police work—is surrounding a house with a single man holed up inside. Soldiers, on the other hand, rarely work in units smaller than a squad. The paratrooper who killed Ernest Roquemore this night—by accident it would seem—was one of the few army men who had been removed from his unit and assigned to a police car. The policeman he was working with wounded a youth and two girls, 13 and 17, with his personal hunting weapon, a 16-gauge shotgun.

Police said they were looking for loot. One of the injured girls had been visiting the apartment of her brother where the shootings took place. Their father is talking.

"My wife was talking to my daughter on the phone when it happened. My wife just heard a shot on the phone. She said, 'John, please, something done happened already. Please go over to Hal's house (which is my son). Somebody's done shot somebody.' I got here as fast as I could and they wouldn't let me in. They said it was looting. There was some looting around the corner, but my son, he don't believe in looting. Like they said that furniture was looted. But that furniture wasn't looted. I've got to pay. I've got the receipt. My son put $800 down on that furniture and he still owes $592. They wouldn't let him get it because he owes for an automobile. So I had to co-sign for him. I got the book here. We paid regular. They said he had to put that heavy payment down for the furniture.

"They said there was somebody in there with a gun. Maybe there was, but I didn't see him. Then they said they was some marijuana. I don't know."

Roquemore, 19, a resident of the building, was shot accidentally while the paratrooper was firing at an armed youth who was running away. He was not caught, but police said they found a packet of marijuana on the stairs.

The father continued: "They just bust in there without saying nothing to nobody. Now I come over here and they won't tell me anything. They said, 'Well, you can't go in there.' I said, 'Why not? I want to see who's hurt because my son stays here. I want to see what's the matter.' They said, 'Naw, you have to stay on the side.' Then this Negro soldier, he said, 'Look, do like they say. Don't get yourself involved. Take it easy. So many of my people getting killed already.' I stood back there. I obeyed them. Then I waited and they tried to take the furniture out. I got the book right here. I'm waiting for them now. They can't take that furniture out because it belongs to my son.

"I don't know about that marijuana or that looting or what. I don't see where that give them the right to be shooting when they come in the house. They should find out who's *in there* first.

"There's four people shot. They said somebody had a gun. But didn't nobody up there shoot at nobody. Maybe they thought somebody was breaking in and then if I had a gun I might get it out. But the policemen didn't say nothing. They just came in shooting.

"This is worser than the thing, the raid, that started the riots. Didn't nobody do nothing but they just go in there shooting. Then they want to say, 'How come the colored man get down wrong?' That make any man do something wrong."

The institution of the booster, the organizer, is a familiar one. One corporation front man I know introduces himself as "the vice president in charge of joining good causes." The adherents of this institution—which include the Babbitt, the PR man, the associate minister, and other assorted icon polishers—have generally been hired for their winning smiles and friction-free personalities.

More recently, the institution has been enlivened by a band of men who neither smile much nor avoid friction. Although Detroit may have been a little behind other cities, it is now home to a number of black community organizers. These men saw the riots as an opportunity to assert leadership in building a community. They were excited by the riots and proud of them in a way, but they were also depressed at the implication that rioting might present more opportunities than community organization.

Frank Ditto came to Detroit from Chicago just a month before the riots to work for a new group called CESSA, Churches on the East Side for Social Action. He was in Newark at the Black Power convention when the riots broke out in Detroit. He had gained fame in Chicago as the leader of 150 consecutive days of miles-long marches through the streets, ending each night at the home of Mayor Richard J. Daley. One of the first friends Ditto made in Detroit was Rennie Freeman, the executive director of the West Community Organization, an older counterpart to CESSA in the area that was most seriously hit by the riots. Whenever Ditto and Freeman meet they give one another the Black-Power secret grip, a variation on Indian wrestling.

Freeman was working on 12th Street when the riot began to emerge. John Conyers, the Negro Democrat who represents the West Side in Congress, asked Freeman to help quiet the crowds shortly before noon on Sunday. Freeman tells the story:

"Conyers and his functionaries came down here talking to me saying, 'Will you help?' I said, 'Man, I'll help you if you do the right thing.' He said, 'Well, I'm going to get a bullhorn down here and get these cats off the streets. We don't want anybody hurt.' So I said no. He said, 'What are you doing down here then? What are you here for? Do you want a riot?' You've got all these brothers down on the street corner and as I told Conyers, 'If you go up and down 12th Street with a bullhorn trying to tell all the colored folks to get off *their* street when these cops are standing out here with shotguns and bayonets, what's going to happen is that the people are going to turn against *you*.' I said I'd help if the police were going to get out, too, but I think even at that point it was too late. The young brothers was out there and they didn't dig it *at all*.

"I started walking down the street with the cat and here I am with John on one side and this functionary on the other. I said to myself, 'Well, hell, I'm not walking down here with these armband Negroes. What do I look like riding up and down 12th Street telling these cats to get off the street with these functionaries? John just can't comprehend that the disorganized brothers have something to say. He thinks that if you aren't organized you have nothing to say. So he made the mistake, but at that he was the only cat down there. None of these other Negro politicians was there. Conyers was the only one."

Regardless of the difficulty of organizing the "disorganized brothers," both Ditto and Freeman place their faith in organization. Said Ditto, "To be honest with myself, having been oppressed and subjected to all the dehumanizing factors of American life as a black man, I very well could have been out there burning, looting, and sniping. I see more point in organizing than I do in looting. It's more constructive. This kind of thing here, the rioting, runs out of gas in four or five days. With an organization when you get weak and tired you know that you have someone beside you who you can lean up against and still keep going on."

Ditto's mood varied widely. In an interview given a television reporter while the riots were still going on, organization, except in a special sense, was not foremost in his mind.

"Is this organized or a spontaneous thing?" the reporter asked.

"It's a combination of both. It was spontaneous in the sense that it was caused by just another incident of police brutality. It was organized in the sense that it has been going on more than four hundred years and the black folks have been organized for four hundred years to fight for survival."

He was even willing during the riots to take a real-politik view of the loss of Negro lives and property in the riot.

"The way that society looks at these things, we would say it's unfortunate, but the United States is dropping napalm bombs on women and children over in Viet Nam and no one has anything to say about it. I mean, this is a state of war. This is the price of war. You might get killed and I might get killed and who gives a damn?"

A few days later, Ditto encountered two young hustlers who had enjoyed the rioting, but who were unwilling to extract any political moral from it.

"If they wanted to do something, really wanted to cut it up, why did they do it down here," one said. "In all these soup lines and burned apartments up and down 12th Street, all I see is colored people in a fix. They should have gone up to Grosse Pointe. Get in their cars and go up there and riot. That'd show somebody something. Not like this; this didn't show the white people nothing."

Organization was not for the hustlers. "The white man's got everything," one said. "I'd like to get in on it but I can't get in on it so I get around it. What's the old saying, 'God bless the child that's got his own'? The Negroes have just got to get out and get theirs like I'm getting mine. Let them go for theirself."

Ditto didn't like it. "Do you realize that just 150 years ago when black babies were born and brought into the earth the slave master would snatch them away from their mother and send them off to some other plantation as soon as they were old enough? They separated brothers and sisters and fathers and sons. Negroes don't stick together because of the psychological brainwashing they've been through for hundreds of years."

"I'll tell you one thing," the hustler replied. "It would have been hard to get me over here at all if my brother in Africa hadn't been selling me for some beads."

Despite this sort of apathy, Ditto and Freeman were planning to try to bring together young Negroes like these—and others even tougher and less articulate—with the hope of formulating a program of police-community relations. Freeman explained, "We've got to strike while the iron is hot. Right now nobody knows what the hell to do. But the brothers can tell them what to do without hesitating. The brothers know what needs to be done.

"They aren't going to hear it from these Uncle Tom preachers. They don't even know what the *gossip* is on

12th Street. This is the time to organize. Everybody's together if you leave out the Toms. The Negroes in the community belong to what's happening, man. Those rioters was running down the streets and I see these middle class people standing out on the porches giving the Black Power sign. You know, women in house dresses giving the fist. And it is clear that this thing about the lower class being disenchanted is bullshit. Negroes are disenchanted. It's not just the cats that have got the guts to throw the bricks that's pissed off. Everybody is pissed off. There these chicks are that sit on the PTA boards giving the Black Power sign when there's smoke all around. Even the Toms break down and cry. They just don't have no goddam guts. That's the only difference."

This was on one of their hopeful days. The next day, after attending the funeral of a Negro youth apparently killed by police during the rioting, Ditto's mood was one of despair. "I've had people treat me like that cigaret butt there just because I'm black. I could very easily be on the other side of the street with a 30-30 rifle. I have this fight with myself every day. I keep having this hope that people will somehow come to their senses. I don't know what I'll be doing a year from now. I might give up on this organizing. I just don't know what I'll do."

September 1967

Open Letter on
White Justice and the Riots

LEE RAINWATER

A great deal of the difficulty in understanding what causes riots and what might be done about them comes from a misunderstanding of exactly what their nature is. A riot seems almost always to begin with an incident in which the police make an effort at enforcing one or another law—whether the culprits involved be a tipsy driver, a traffic law violator, or the operators and patrons of a blind pig. In other words, riots grow out of efforts at social control where society's officials move in on behavior which the informal social controls of the community do not prove sufficient to contain.

As the police go about their business, a curious crowd gathers. The crowd watches what is going on and reflects on it, and some members come to deny the legitimacy of what the police are doing. Rather than responding with satisfaction to the smooth functioning of the social control forces, the crowd members respond with anger and resentment; they identify with the culprits rather than with the law. This identification often takes the form of a belief either that the culprits are innocent, or that they're being treated more roughly than is warranted or just.

The riot develops from this initial incident as the people in the crowd begin to express their anger in response to the situation—they throw rocks at the police, or make attempts to rescue the prisoners. Here they are only acting out the strong and unpleasant emotions stimulated by what they see and the meanings they assign to it. But as this process continues and people talk to each other about what has happened, the matter becomes more ideological— that is, the events are interpreted in an increasingly larger context. The incident becomes an example of a society in which whites do as they please, while Negroes are held accountable for every minor infraction, even those infractions involving behavior that is not really voluntary. For example, a man may get drunk because he is depressed and discouraged about his situation, or he may spend his time on the streets and get in trouble there because he has given up looking for a job. The fury of the rioters is probably exacerbated by their weariness at trying to manage their lives in such a way that they can avoid the attentive ministrations of the social control agents (and these include truant officers, welfare investigators, and personnel officers, as well as the police).

By now the guilt or innocence of the culprits, and the manner in which the police treat them, are no longer that central. Instead, the focus is on the crowd members' general feelings that they live in a world in which they are constantly held accountable to standards of justice which are not applied to others. They feel that the merchants with whom they deal cheat them, that employers are either indifferent or exploiting toward them, that the police are disrespectful and suspicious of them. Therefore, they feel that the police (as representatives of the society at large) are perpetrating the greater evil—an evil by comparison with which the minor peccadillos of the drunken driver, traffic violator, the blind-pig patron are, in human terms, irrelevant.

Further, as incidents like this multiply, and as sophistication about Negro victimization rises in the ghetto community, it becomes increasingly possible to generalize this process without a particular incident. Following the news of the Newark, Detroit, and East Harlem riots in July, a group of Negro teenagers went on a rampage after a rock and roll concert, smashing and looting several of New York's Fifth Avenue stores. They did not need the provocation of an actual encounter with the police to touch off this vivid rejection of legal authority.

A riot is a social event which provides different opportunities to different participants. It is a short-lived "opportunity structure." Of all the aspects of the riot, this is the least well understood. There is no single "rioter," but rather many kinds of activities, each contributing a little bit to make up the total event. We know almost nothing about who takes each of the possible roles in the rioting— looter, sniper, police attacker, sympathetic bystander, ideological interpreter, and so on. It does seem that the most popular category is that of looter. This makes sense; what the rioters are saying, more than anything else, is "we haven't gotten our share." On Detroit's East and West sides the furniture and appliance stores seemed the hardest hit. "Big ticket" items are the proof of the affluent society and the looters knew exactly where to find them. In this respect the riots become a kind of primitive effort at an income redistribution which the society refuses to support in any lawful and regularized way.

The snipers, on the other hand, we can only vaguely understand. Indeed, the evidence seems to suggest that snipers are more often phantom than real; a very few snipers (perhaps none at all) are necessary to legitimate the belief of police and National Guardsmen that they are "at war" and that the danger is so great that they may fire with impunity into the rioting community. In Detroit, one such phantom sniper was apparently responsible for the National Guard machine-gunning a "white" motel near the General Motors building and inadvertently hitting an out-of-town woman staying there.

Riots are difficult to control precisely because of this voluntary division of labor among the participants. Because their many different sorts of activities require different sorts of responses, the riot becomes a highly complex event that can be brought under control only by a mass show of force (or perhaps by a show of no force at all). This, plus the fact that once the riot gets under way there is almost total denial of legitimacy to the police, means that the area must be *occupied* to be controlled—a process that calls ever further into question the legitimacy of the total society and its laws. The riots elicit from the official world exactly the kind of behavior that confirms the ghetto's estimate of white justice. The trigger-happy behavior of the National Guard and the police and the haphazard way in which arrests are or are not made deepens the conviction that being accorded justice depends more on luck than on the rule of law. The rising hysteria of the fatigued and frightened men in uniform seems to release all of their latent hostility to Negroes. In New Jersey, Los Angeles, and numerous smaller cities the civilian officials have hardly behaved better; it is to the credit of Detroit's Mayor Cavanaugh and his cabinet that no hint of such prejudice and bitterness has been apparent there.

Riots, then, provide different kinds of ghetto dwellers with different opportunities to pursue highly varied goals. The larger the riots get, the easier for individuals to become participants, and probably the more varied the goals they pursue.

In this context, it's quite clear from the data on the social characteristics of those arrested and convicted in Watts that the rioters are probably *not* exclusively "young hoodlums." For example, over half of those arrested in Watts were twenty-five years of age and over and as many as 40 percent were over thirty. Further, about two-thirds of those arrested and convicted were employed. It is certainly true that those arrested were very familiar with the law; less than 30 percent of them had no prior arrest. This, however, is not evidence that they are criminals, but only that they live in the ghetto. (Note, for example, that half of those arrested had never been convicted.) We would need more precise data to know what differences there might be between those who form some kind of active core of the rioters and those who take part more casually, by minor looting and the like. It might well be that the active core is more youthful and more solidly involved in delinquent activity than the others. But the most important fact here is that one could not make a riot of any size with the dominant proportion of the participants composed only of "young hoodlums."

There should be no mistake on this point. A very large proportion of the able-bodied members of any lower class Negro ghetto are potential participants in a riot. And, the riot has an ideological meaning for them; it is not simply a diversion which allows for criminal activity. The man who steals a six-pack of beer or breaks a store window does it not out of "criminal" motivation (it would hardly be worth his while), but because he is expressing some important feelings about his world and trying to put these feelings "on the record." If in the process he can derive some material benefit, like a television set or a new G.E. range, that is all to the good because it makes his point even clearer. Everyone in America knows that money talks. The greater the damage in terms of the financial cost of the looting and burning, the more effectively the point has been made.

But just as a riot provides a wide range of opportunities, it also involves a wide range of costs—primarily those of being killed, arrested, or burned out. It is probably true that stable working class Negroes (who are often as much prisoners of the ghetto as lower class people) are much less interested in the opportunities of riots and more concerned about the costs. They often share the feeling that legal authority is neither just nor fair, but they also have material possessions and social positions to protect. They don't want their homes burned by rioters or strafed by the National Guard. And they are concerned that their children will become involved in the riot—that they will be treated as, and may come to think of themselves as, the "young hoodlums."

Because this more stable working class in the ghetto usually supplies its "community leaders," there is real danger that any investigating committee will be misled into believing that the riots represent the feelings of only a small minority. These "respectable" spokesmen for the area must not be allowed (no matter how honest their personal views might be) to mislead an investigating group in its analysis of the nature of riot participation.

There is always deep conflict and ambivalence in the ghetto over the issue of police protection versus police harassment. The ghetto is a dangerous place for its inhabitants, and they would like to have firm and competent police surveillance. On the other hand, that very surveillance carries with it the danger of unjust and unseemly behavior by the police. Police rationality dictates that anyone in the ghetto is more suspect of crime than anyone in a white middle class neighborhood. From the police point of view, then, ghetto residents should be more willing to cooperate by answering questions and accepting arrest. The conflict built into this kind of situation can perhaps be somewhat ameliorated by more integrated police forces, and by vigorous supervision of the police to see that they are not impolite or overly aggressive. But that is no real solution to the problem.

Further, riots may well become more frequent and larger as time goes on due to the diffusion of knowledge, almost technical in nature, about how a riot is carried on. It is not too fanciful to say that anyone who watches television and reads the newspapers learns from the coverage of Watts, Hough, Newark, Harlem, and Detroit how to participate in a riot. Therefore, *without any organization at all* in the sense of a command structure, people in all parts of the nation know what to do and what roles one might take should a riot opportunity present itself. Millions of Americans today could, on request, fashion Molotov cocktails, who a year or two ago would not have known the meaning of the term. Similarly, millions of Americans now know that many rioters are not arrested and that snipers are seldom caught. There is no way of preventing the diffusion of this knowledge; we can only try to prevent the need and willingness to use it.

Finally, the particular quality of the riots reflects the Negro cultural emphasis on expressivity over instrumentality—practical, goal-directed action. A WASP riot under similar conditions would probably be a much more hard-nosed and certainly much more bloody and violent event. The "carnival atmosphere" noted by observers at all major riots is probably a direct reflection of the expressive emphasis in all group activity among Negroes, whether it be church participation, the blues, a rock and roll concert, or street corner banter.

This is perhaps also part of the key to why the riots seem to be relatively unorganized, both locally and nationally. Discussion of an organized national conspiracy is probably a white projection. Whites find it very difficult to understand why Negroes aren't more efficient in their rebellion—why there is no national cadre, no command structure, no greater efficiency in doing damage. A good part of this may be because this is not the Negroes' preferred way of going about things. Rather, in the midst of an ineffable group solidarity, a kind of free enterprise prevails in which each individual works for himself, perhaps cooperating for short periods of time with others to accomplish some immediate goals, but in the main doing things his own way as an expression of his own feelings. The expressive focus may be very important in formulating an ideology, and thus ultimately have a strong effect on the frequency and nature of rioting. But, that effect is achieved not by *organization,* but rather through *communication* of a developing social doctrine.

Negro expressiveness may also account for the tremendous disjunction between the verbal communication of supposedly violent groups such as RAM and spokesmen for violence like H. Rap Brown, and the fact that organized paramilitary action seems to be virtually absent from the riots. They behave as if they were designed more for display to the white press and titillated or scandalized Negro audiences than for actual committed revolutionary action. I don't think this point about Negro expressive life style is particularly important in understanding or accounting for the riots except to the extent that it helps us understand and get behind the myths that some whites (particularly Senators Eastland and McClellan, the press, and law enforcement agencies) and some Negroes (like Carmichael in Havana) are putting forth.

When we seek the basic causes of the riots the central question is: Why are there so many Negroes for whom riots provide an opportunity for meaningful self-expression and gain? Further, why are the opportunities sought in such situations so destructive of social order? We know that in other situations which provide technical opportunity, for example, blackouts, nothing of the sort happens, although the authorities always fear that it might.

Much of the popular interpretation of riots has turned on an understanding of the really desperate situation of the worst off in the ghettos, of those who make up the "underclass," which may include anywhere between one-third and one-half of the ghetto population. Again, however, the figures on the Watts arrestees are instructive. Two-thirds of the men arrested and convicted were employed and perhaps as many as one-third of them were earning over $300 a month. Forty percent (or over half of those who had ever been married) were living with their spouses. Thus, when a riot takes place, a significant portion even of those above the poverty line may well be drawn into participation. This should alert us to the fact that rioting is not exclusively a problem of poverty as currently defined.

One may talk about two major kinds of causative factors—one involving *class* (by which is meant simply economic deprivation and all of the cultural and social consequences that flow from it) and the other involving the inferior *caste* position of Negroes to whites. This latter factor is most directly expressed in ghetto hostility toward the police, but it is also involved in the attack the riots come to represent on the total white-dominated society. Even the Negro who is well off in class terms may feel a strong pull toward participation if he has had the experience of being interrogated and perhaps arrested in a ghetto area simply because his face is black. Where men have little to protect and where their experience of hostility and indifference from the white world is even more pervasive, as in the case of the lower class, the resistance to participation will be even less.

The fact that even a significant minority of the participants are members of seemingly stable families earning above poverty level incomes tells us something about what is involved in exclusion from ordinary American society in a city as prosperous as Detroit or Los Angeles. Whatever poverty as minimum subsistence may mean, it is quite clear that people with incomes as high as $5,000 a year are really not able to feel that they participate in the broad spectrum of average American affluence and satisfaction. A community in which the great majority of the families must exist on significantly less than the median family income for the nation is a community of failures. Inclusion in such a community, compounded as it is by belonging to a historically excluded group and the knowledge that there is a connection between racial exclusion and economic exclusion, is undesirable to those who live within its confines as well as to those outside.

Thus, the ghetto community has few informal social

controls; people tend to minimize trouble by avoiding each other more than by building up informal social networks which ensure observance of common group standards. Everybody does pretty much what he wants as long as he can stay out of the clutches of the authorities. Thus, the individual has few effective sanctions available at the informal level. Even those who disapprove of rioting are powerless to do much about it by informally punishing those who participate. Any influence they might have is vitiated by the common perception of all that the authorities are just about as unjust as the law-breakers. Ghetto residents will, in desperation, call upon officialdom to punish those of their fellows who are directly making trouble for them, but they do it in much the same way that one might pay the neighborhood bully to discipline an enemy. The bully is called upon because of his power, not because of any legitimate authority.

The riots bring into high relief the ever present schism in the Negro community between those who feel they have nothing to lose, and those who want to protect what they have—while the former riot, the latter deluge the police and mayor's office with telephone calls demanding protection from the rioters, demanding that the riot be put down before their homes are burned, their community destroyed. The physical contrast in Detroit is particularly striking. Not three blocks from the 12th Street riot area are substantial homes on well-maintained tree-lined streets. Their residents, like other stable working and middle class Negro Detroiters, wanted the riots put down with all possible dispatch; the potential cost of getting even with Whitey was too great.

And then there are the Negro businessmen in the ghetto —the "soul brothers." Detroit's Grand River Boulevard, where the riot-damaged buildings string out for miles, has a great many soul brothers (and one soul mother) whose quickly inscribed signs protected them from damage while on either side the looting or burning seemed complete. But, one can't count the "soul brother" signs that are no longer there because the glass was broken; and an occasional sign is still observable when only one broken show window in a soul brother's store was required to accomplish the looting. The signs obviously provided some protection, but exactly how much they lower the risk is a moot point. If the protection is very high, it would suggest that the hostility of the more prosperous and respectable Negroes is not returned by the rioters; if protection is low the rioters might be saying, as those in Bedford-Stuyvesant are reported to have taunted Negro policemen, "Take off your black masks so we can see your white faces."

Summing up: (1) the root cause of the riots lies in a caste system deeply imbedded in our society that has created a situation in which (a) a very large proportion of Negroes are denied the opportunity to achieve an average American standard of living, and (b) even those Negroes who do, by dint of their own efforts, manage to come reasonably close to an average American standard are still subjected to special disabilities and insults because of their confinement to a ghetto community. (2) From the immediate point of view of the rioters, the most pervasive factor which prevents their achieving some sense of a decent life is that of living in poverty or near-poverty (as a rough rule from, say, having incomes less than one-half to two-thirds that of the median family income for the nation). This economic exclusion affects almost everything they do —their ability to purchase all those elements that make up the "standard package" that most American families deem their right. And the inability to earn more than this kind of poverty or near-poverty income affects the respect they are able to elicit from their own family members, members of their immediate community, and from the society at large.

It seems likely that the starting mechanisms for a riot are fairly dependent on the existence of pronounced poverty coupled with very high rates of unemployment. This, at least, would seem to be important to the extent that young men (say men under twenty-five) have a disproportionate influence on getting a riot going. This group is excluded not only from the availability of something like an average American life, but is excluded even within its own community. The older men do tend to be employed and to earn incomes reasonably close to the poverty line. It is the younger men in the ghetto who are most completely and dramatically excluded from any participation in the conventional rewards of the society.

If this diagnosis is correct—that the direct cause of participation in the riots (as opposed to the precipitating incidents) is economic marginality—it should put us on notice that no "community action" programs, whether they involve better police-community relations or rapprochement with the new black militant leaders, will prevent riots. Rather, the necessary condition for any permanent solution to the riot problem will be to provide a reasonable approximation of the "average American standard of living" for every family. This means managing the society so that poverty and near-poverty are eliminated. Only then can those who now participate in and support the riots find themselves in situations where rioting has become a meaningless, useless activity. This "income strategy" has two principal elements.

The more important of these is creating work. The demand for goods and services must be manipulated in such a way that private and public employers have more jobs which they are willing to offer to relatively unskilled and "undesirable" employees because they need these employees to satisfy the demands for their products. This is the aggregate demand solution to poverty argued by James Tobin, Hyman Minsky, and others. Such a solution has the advantage that it makes maximum use of what is already our main technique for distributing goods and services to families—that is, employment. A further advantage is that an aggregate demand, full employment situation tends to upgrade wages in low wage industries and thus alleviate the problem of near-poverty and poverty among employed workers.

An integral part of this strategy will probably have to be some direct planning by the government to make demand for unskilled workers roughly equal to that for more skilled workers. The most promising suggestions in this area involve the "new careers for the poor" proposals which create new kinds of jobs and avenues for advancement in public service activities. But it is very important that these programs not be developed as programs of "last resort employment," but rather as permanent programs which are productive for the entire society.

It might be well to design crash programs, as well as possible subsidized employment in private industry, for young workers. Such crash programs would be a dead end, however, unless they were part of an overall aggregate demand plus special-programs-for-unskilled-workers strategy.

It follows that the government agencies who should be responsible for solving the problems of the riots are not so much HEW, Labor, and OEO, as they are the Treasury Department, Council of Economic Advisors, and the

Federal Reserve Board. OEO-type programs such as the Job Corps, which are designed only to train a small number of lower class individuals to compete more successfully within a system that offers them little or no opportunity as long as they remain unskilled, cannot hope to solve the massive income problems of the whole disadvantaged sector. Unless the power and skills of those agencies which set basic fiscal and economic policy are brought to bear (and backed, of course, by a committed President) it is very difficult to believe that we can solve the problem of rioting—or the more general problem of poverty, and the racial caste system it supports.

The second aspect of the income strategy will involve some form of guaranteed minimum income. We now know that the various particular plans that have been suggested —negative income tax, family allowance, upgraded welfare systems, and the like—all represent variations on a common system of income redistribution (see the work of Christopher Green recently published by The Brookings Institution). The important issue is not so much which of these plans is best as what the guaranteed minimum is to be and what the tax rate on the subsidy is to be. Given the amount of current research activity on income maintenance, the basic technical issues involved in a guaranteed income program will be resolved in the next two or three years. The real question is how we are to muster the political goodwill to put a program into effect.

A guaranteed minimum income program will be crucial for two reasons. First of all, there will always be families for whom the economy cannot provide a reasonable income on a regular and secure basis. Perhaps more important from a political point of view, a national commitment to a guaranteed minimum income will spur the government to maintain employment as fully as possible so that the

maximum number of people will derive the maximum proportion of their incomes from their own earnings and not
from the national dole. The political vulnerability of any
group which over a long period of time derives a significant proportion of its income from government transfers
will always be great. Therefore, income maintenance plans
can only be a form of family insurance and national political insurance, not a major way of channeling income to
families.

A solution to the Negro income problem is thus the
sine qua non for a permanent solution to the problem of
rioting. With this achieved, tremendous pressure will be
generated to move out of the ghetto. I would guess that
only a small minority of current ghetto residents would
prefer to stay, given a choice. This pressure will itself facilitate the development of desegregated housing; but the
government must also facilitate the dispersion of ghetto
residents to a more integrated life away from the central
city ghettos. That dispersion would to some extent be aided
by fair housing laws, but perhaps more important would
be the development of government-supported programs for
the expansion of middle and lower middle income housing.
This would maximize the range of choice available to anyone seeking a better place to live.

It is my belief that it will prove impossible to solve the
many other problems of the ghetto until the income problem is solved. Further, I believe that these other problems
—education, health, political participation, and the like—
would be amenable to very different and much simpler
solutions if the Negro families involved had decent incomes.

The ideological developments of the past ten years in
connection with the situation of the Negro American pose
a challenge to the government and to white society generally. Depending on how this challenge is met, we will move

more slowly or more quickly toward the basic economic solutions offered above. I see the vague and often contradictory militant civil rights ideology which has developed over the past few years as a result of two factors. First, as the nation has become more prosperous, it has become increasingly obvious that it is not necessary to have a deprived and excluded group in our midst. The dynamics of affluence themselves call into question the old caste-like racial arrangements. As some Negroes participate in that prosperity, and as they look on the tremendous affluence of white society, there is a strong push in the direction of forcing the society to accord Negroes their share. This factor was perhaps the dominant influence in the early period of the new civil rights consciousness that started in the early '60's— suddenly it seemed ridiculous to most Americans that anyone should be excluded when we have so much.

Second, and more recently, has come a new wave of black populism. The common theme running through many of the ideas of the new black militants is that Negroes have a right to their own future and their own place in the sun, not just in economic terms but as full men in society. The emphasis on blackness is a reaction to the price that white society seems to want to exact for economic payoffs, a price that seems to involve a denial of oneself as Negro and to require a tame imitation of whatever the going definition of the proper white person is. Now there is a lot of nonsense these days about what Negro culture involves and what black autonomy might mean. But, at the core of the black populist movement is a denial of the right of whites to define who the Negro is and what he may become. This is not only healthy, but much more realistic than the earlier, simple-minded integrationist myth that dominated civil rights activity for so long.

There are now, and will probably continue to be for

some time, conflicts between moving toward the economic goals of the civil rights movement and the black populist goals. The political challenge for white society is to thread its way through these conflicts without denying the validity of either factor, and to select those areas in which the government can further the Negro goals (to my mind, principally the economic area) and those areas in which the main effort at constructing a new social reality will have to be made primarily by Negroes themselves.

The danger here is that the reaction to the black populist goals on the part of the government and whites generally will be so hostile that Negro leaders who emphasize such aims will be progressively alienated and provoked into activities destructive to both sets of goals. In the main, however, the mutual alienation and viciousness that has tended to dominate the civil rights-white power structure dialogue for the past two years is more a result of the government's unwillingness to make major economic commitments than it is of any inherent tendencies in the black populist movement.

In short, the government cannot give Negroes a black culture or a black consciousness, but it can manage the society in such a way as to give them a "black affluence." If the government does not do what it can do, then we can only expect the courageous and the committed in the Negro community to become more aggressive and more destructive toward the larger society which has the necessary means, but refuses to use them.

September 1967

Sniping...
A New Pattern of Violence?

TERRY ANN KNOPF

On July 23, 1968, at 2:15 P.M., Cleveland's Mayor, Carl B. Stokes, who was in Washington, D.C., that day, made what he expected to be a routine telephone call to his office back home. He was told of information from military, F.B.I., and local police intelligence sources indicating that an armed uprising by black militants was scheduled to take place at 8 A.M. the next day. According to the reports, Ahmed Evans, a militant leader who headed a group called the Black Nationalists of New Libya, planned to drive to Detroit that night to secure automatic weapons. There were further reports that Evans' followers had already purchased bandoliers, ammunition pouches, and first-aid kits that same day. Simultaneous uprisings were reportedly being planned for Detroit, Pittsburgh, and Chicago.

At 6 P.M., in response to these reports, several unmarked police cars were assigned to the area of Evans' house. At about 8:20 P.M. a group of armed men, some of whom were wearing bandoliers of ammunition, emerged from the house. Almost at once, an intense gun battle broke out between the police and the armed men, lasting for roughly an hour. A second gun battle between the police and snipers broke out shortly after midnight about 40 blocks away. In the wake of these shoot-outs, sporadic looting and firebombing erupted and continued for several days. By the time the disorder was over, 16,400 National Guardsmen had been mobilized, at least nine persons had been killed (including three policemen), while the property damage was estimated at $1.5 million. Police listed most of their casualties as "shot by sniper."

Immediately, the Cleveland tragedy was described as a deliberate plot against the police and said to signal a new phase in the current course of racial conflict. *The Cleveland Press* (July 24, 1968) compared the violence in Cleveland to guerrilla activity in Saigon and noted: ". . . It didn't seem to be a Watts, or a Detroit, or a Newark. Or even a Hough of two years ago. No, this tragic night seemed to be part of a plan." Thomas A. Johnson writing in *The New York Times* (July 28, 1968) stated: ". . . It marks perhaps the first documented case in recent history of black, armed, and organized violence against the police."

As the notion that police were being "ambushed" took hold in the public's mind, many observers reporting on the events in Cleveland and similar confrontations in other cities, such as Gary, Peoria, Seattle, and York, Pennsylvania, emphasized that the outbreaks had several prominent features in common.

The first was the element of planning. Racial outbursts have traditionally been spontaneous affairs, without organization and without leadership. While no two disorders are similar in every respect, studies conducted in the past have indicated that a riot is a dynamic process that goes through stages of development. John P. Spiegel of Brandeis' Lemberg Center for the Study of Violence, has discerned four stages in the usual sort of rioting: the precipitating event, street confrontation, "Roman holiday," and seige. A sequence of stages is outlined in somewhat similar terms in the section of the Kerner Report on "the riot process." It is significant, however, that neither the Lemberg Center nor the Kerner Commission found any evidence of an organized plan or "conspiracy" in civil disorders prior to 1968. According to the Kerner Report: ". . . The Commission has found no evidence that all or any of the disorders or the incidents that led to them were planned or directed by any organization or group—international, national, or local."

Since the Cleveland shoot-out, however, many observers have suggested that civil disorders are beginning to take a new form, characterized by some degree of planning, organization, and leadership.

The second new feature discerned in many of 1968's summer outbreaks was the attacks on the police. In the past, much of the racial violence that occurred was directed at property rather than persons. Cars were stoned, stores were looted, business establishments were firebombed, and residences, in some instances, were damaged or destroyed. However, since the Cleveland gun battle, there have been suggestions that policemen have become the primary targets of violence. A rising curve of ambushes of the police was noted in the October 7, 1968 issue of the *U.S. News & World Report* which maintained that at least 8 policemen were killed and 47 wounded in such attacks last summer.

Finally, attacks on the police are now said to be *regularly* characterized by hit-and-run sniping. Using either home-made weapons or commercial and military weapons, such as automatics, bands of snipers are pictured initiating guerrilla warfare in our cities.

This view of the changing nature of racial violence can be found across a broad spectrum of the press, ranging from the moderately liberal *New York Times* to the militantly rightist *American Opinion.* On August 3, 1968, *The New York Times* suggested in an editorial:

. . . The pattern in 1967 has not proved to be the pattern of 1968. Instead of violence almost haphazardly exploding, it has sometimes been deliberately planned. And while the 1967 disorders served to rip away false facades of racial progress and expose rusting junkyards of broken promises, the 1968 disorders also reveal a festering militancy that prompts some to resort to open warfare.

Shortly afterward (August 14, 1968), *Crime Control Digest,* a biweekly periodical read by many law-enforcement officials across the country, declared:

The pattern of civil disorders in 1968 has changed from the pattern that prevailed in 1967, and the elaborate U.S. Army, National Guard and police riot control program prepared to meet this year's "long hot summer" will have to be changed if this year's type of civil disturbance is to be prevented or controlled.

This year's riot tactics have featured sniping and hit-and-run attacks on the police, principally by Black Power extremists, but by teen-agers in an increasing number of instances. The type of crimes being committed by the teen-agers and the vast increase in their participation has already brought demands that they be tried and punished as adults.

On September 13, 1968, *Time* took note of an "ominous trend" in the country:

Violence as a form of Negro protest appears to be changing from the spontaneous combustion of a mob to the premeditated shoot-outs of a far-out few. Many battles have started with well-planned sniping at police.

Predictably, the November 1968 issue of *American Opinion* went beyond the other accounts by linking reported attacks on the police to a Communist plot:

The opening shots of the Communists' long-planned terror offensive against our local police were fired in Cleveland on the night of July 23, 1968, when the city's Glenville area rattled with the scream of automatic weapons. . . . What happened in Cleveland, alas, was only a beginning.

To further emphasize the point, a large headline crying "terrorism" was included on the cover of the November issue.

Despite its relative lack of objectivity, *American Opinion* is the only publication that has attempted to list sniping incidents. Twenty-five specific instances of attacks on police were cited in the November issue. Virtually every other publication claiming a change in the nature of racial violence pointing to the "scores of American cities" affected and the "many battles" between blacks and the police has confined itself to a few perfunctory examples as evidence. Even when a few examples have been offered, the reporters usually have not attempted to investigate and confirm them.

Without attempting an exhaustive survey, we at the Lemberg Center were able to collect local and national press clippings, as well as wire-service stories, that described 25 separate incidents of racial violence in July and

August of last summer. In all these stories, sniping was alleged to have taken place at some point or other in the fracas, and in most of them, the police were alleged to have been the primary targets of the sharpshooters. Often, too, the reports held that evidence had been found of planning on the part of "urban guerrillas," and at times it was claimed that the police had been deliberately ambushed. Needless to say, the specter of the Black Panthers haunts a number of the accounts. Throughout, one finds such phrases as these: "snipers hidden behind bushes . . . ," "isolated sniper fire . . . ," "scattered sniping directed at the police . . . ," "exchange of gunfire between snipers and police . . . ," "snipers atop buildings in the area. . . ." It is small wonder that the rewrite men at *Time* and other national magazines discerned a new and sinister pattern in the events of that summer. Small wonder that many concerned observers are convinced that the country's racial agony has entered a new phase of deliberate covert violence.

But how valid is this sometimes conspiratorial, sometimes apocalyptic view? What is the evidence for it, apart from these newspaper accounts?

Our assessment is based on an analysis of newspaper clippings, including a comparison of initial and subsequent reports, local and national press coverage, and on telephone interviews with high-ranking police officials. The selection of police officials was deliberate on our part. In the absence of city or state investigations of most of the incidents, police departments were found to be the best (and in many cases the only) source of information. Moreover, as the reported targets of sniping, police officials understandably had a direct interest in the subject.

Of course, the selection of this group did involve an element of risk. A tendency of some police officials to exaggerate and inflate sniping reports was thought to be unavoidable. We felt, though, that every group involved would have a certain bias and that in the absence of interviewing every important group in the cities, the views of police officials were potentially the most illuminating and therefore the most useful. Our interviews with them aimed at the following points: 1) evidence of planning; 2) the number of snipers; 3) the number of shots fired; 4) affiliation of the sniper or snipers with an organization; 5) statistical breakdowns of police and civilian casualties by sniping; and 6) press coverage of the incident.

As the press reports showed, a central feature in the scheme of those alleging a new pattern involves the notion of planning. Hypothesizing a local (if not national) conspiracy, observers have pictured black militants luring the police to predetermined spots where the policemen become the defenseless victims of an armed attack. No precipitating incident is involved in these cases except perhaps for a false citizen's call.

Despite this view, the information we gathered indicates that at least 17 out of the 25 disorders surveyed (about 70 percent) *did* begin with an identifiable precipitating event (such as an arrest seen by the black community as insulting or unjust) similar to those uncovered for "traditional" disorders. The figure of 70 percent is entirely consistent with the percentage of known precipitating incidents isolated by researchers at the Lemberg Center for past disorders (also about 70 percent).

In Gary, Indiana, the alleged sniping began shortly after two young members of a gang were arrested on charges of rape. In York, Pennsylvania, the violence began after a white man fired a shotgun from his apartment at some blacks on the street. Blacks were reportedly angered upon learning that the police had failed to arrest the gunman. In Peoria, Illinois, police arrested a couple for creating a disturbance in a predominantly black housing-project area. A group of young people then appeared on the scene and began throwing missiles at the police. In Seattle, Washington, a disturbance erupted shortly after a rally was held to protest the arrest of two men at the local Black Panther headquarters. Yet the disorders that followed these incidents are among the most prominently mentioned as examples of planned violence.

Many of the precipitating events were tied to the actions of the police and in some instances they were what the Kerner Commission has referred to as "tension-heightening incidents," meaning that the incident (or the disorder itself) merely crystallized tensions already existing in the community. Shortly before an outbreak in Harvey-Dixmoor, Illinois, on August 6–7, for example, a coroner's jury had ruled that the fatal shooting by police of a young, suspected car thief one month earlier was justifiable homicide. It was the second time in four months that a local policeman had shot a black youth. In Miami, the rally held by blacks shortly before the violence erupted coincided with the Republican National Convention being held about 10 miles away. The crowd was reportedly disappointed when the Reverend Ralph Abernathy and basketball star Wilt Chamberlain failed to appear as announced. In addition, tensions had risen in recent months following increased police canine patrols in the area. Although no immediate precipitating incident was uncovered for the outbreak at Jackson, Michigan on August 5, it is noteworthy that the disorder occurred in front of a Catholic-sponsored center aimed at promoting better race relations, and several weeks earlier, some 30 blacks had attempted to take over the center in the name of "a black group run by black people."

Let us turn briefly to the eight disorders in which triggering events do not appear to have occurred. Despite the absence of such an incident in the Chicago Heights-East Chicago Heights disorder, Chief of Police Robert A. Stone (East Chicago Heights) and Captain Jack Ziegler (Chicago Heights) indicated that they had no evidence of planning and that the disorder was in all probability spontaneous. In particular, Chief Stone indicated that the participants were individuals rather than members of an organization. The same holds true for the "ambuscade" in Brooklyn, New York, which the district attorney said at the time was the work of the Black Panthers. Although no precipitating event was uncovered, R. Harcourt Dodds, Deputy Commissioner for Legal Matters in the New York City Police Department, indicated there was no evidence of planning by anyone or any group. In Jackson, Michigan, as previously noted, tensions in the community had increased in recent weeks prior to the August disorder over a controversial center which some members of the community thought they should control. Thus the absence of precipitating events in at least three cases does not appear to be significant, least of all as evidence of a deliberate conspiracy to kill.

An assessment of the other five cases is considerably more difficult. In Inkster, Michigan, where four nights of isolated sniper fire were reported in August, Chief of Police James L. Fyke did not identify any precipitating event with the disorder and indicated that the state planned to make a case for conspiracy at a forthcoming trial. On the grounds that the two disorders in his city were under police investigation, Lieutenant Norman H. Judd of the Los Angeles Police Department declined comment on possible triggering events. In San Francisco, Chief of Police Thomas J. Cahill said there was evidence of planning. He said that "a firebomb was ignited and the shots were fired as the police vehicle arrived at the scene."

This brings us to Cleveland and Ahmed Evans, the fifth case in this instance. Because of the dramatic nature of the events and the tremendous amount of attention they received in the national press, any findings concerning Cleveland are of utmost importance. It is significant, therefore, that more recent reports have revealed that the July bloodletting was something less than a planned uprising and that the situation at the time was considerably more complicated than indicated initially.

A series of articles appearing in *The New York Times* is instructive. At the time of the disorder, in an account by Thomas A. Johnson, entitled "This Was Real Revolution," *The New York Times* gave strong hints of a plot against the police: "Early indications here were that a small, angry band of Negro men decided to shoot it out with the police. . . ." The article dwelt upon past statements of Ahmed Evans predicting armed uprisings across the nation on May 9, 1967 (they never materialized), rumors of arms caches across the country, and the revolutionary talk of black militants. No mention was made of any precipitating event, nor was there any reference to "tension-heightening incidents" in the community at the time.

One month later, in early September, *The New York Times* published the results of its investigation of the disorder. The report was prepared by three newsmen, all of whom had covered the disorder earlier. Their findings shed new light on the case by suggesting that a series of tension-heightening factors were indeed present in the community at the time of the disorder. For one thing, Mayor Stokes attended a meeting with police officials several hours before the first outbreak and felt that the information about a planned uprising was "probably not correct." Ahmed Evans himself was seen, retrospectively, less as the mastermind of a plot than as just another militant. Anthony Ripley of *The New York Times* wrote of him: "Evans, a tall, former Army Ranger who had been dishonorably discharged after striking an officer, was not regarded as a leading black nationalist. He was an amateur astrologer, 40 years old, given more to angry speeches than to action." Numerous grievances in the community—particularly against the police—which had been overlooked at the time of the disorder, were cited later. For example, it was noted that there were only 165 blacks on a police force of more than 2,000 officers, and there was a deep resentment felt by blacks toward their treatment by the police. The reporters also turned up the fact that in 1966 an investigation committee had given a low professional rating to the police department.

Ahmed Evans himself had some more specific grievances, according to Thomas A. Johnson's follow-up article. He noted that Evans had arranged to rent a vacant tavern for the purpose of teaching the manufacture of African-style clothes and carvings to black youths but that the white landlady had changed her mind. He said that Evans had been further angered upon receiving an eviction order from his home. The Ripley article noted that, two hours before the shooting began, Evans said he had been asleep until his associates informed him that police surveillance cars had been stationed in the area. (Evans was accustomed to posting lookouts on top of buildings.) According to Evans, it was then that the group made the decision to arm.

Did the presence of the police in the area serve to trigger the gun battle that followed? What was the role of the civilian tow-truck driver wearing a police-like uniform? Did his hitching up an old pink Cadillac heighten tensions to the breaking point? Were intelligence reports of a plot in error? Why were arms so readily available to the group? What was the group's intention upon emerging from the house? These questions cannot be answered with any degree of absolute certainty. Nevertheless, it is significant that the earliest interpretations appearing in *The New York Times* were greatly modified by the subsequent articles revealing the complexities of the disorder and suggesting it may have been more spontaneous than planned. As Ripley wrote in his September 2 article:

The Cleveland explosion has been called both an ambush of police and an armed uprising by Negroes. However, the weight of evidence indicates that it was closer to spontaneous combustion.

More recent developments on the controversial Cleveland case deserve mention also. On May 12, 1969, an all-white jury found Ahmed Evans guilty of seven counts of first-degree murder arising out of four slayings during the disorder last July. Evans was sentenced to die in the electric chair on September 22, 1969.

Then, on May 29, 1969, the National Commission on the Causes and Prevention of Violence authorized the release of a report entitled *Shoot-Out in Cleveland; Black Militants and the Police: July 23, 1968* by Louis H. Masotti and Jerome R. Corsi. The report was partially underwritten by the Lemberg Center. Its findings confirmed many of the results of *The Times* investigation and provided additional insights into the case.

Doubt was cast on prior intelligence reports that the Evans group had been assembling an arsenal of handguns and carbines, that Evans planned a trip to Detroit to secure weapons, and that simultaneous outbreaks in other northern cities were planned. ("The truth of these reports was questionable.") Further, it was revealed that these reports came from a single individual and that "other intelligence sources did not corroborate his story." In addition, the Commission report underscored certain provocative actions by the police:

> It was glaringly evident that the police had established a stationary surveillance rather than a moving one. In fact, another surveillance car was facing Ahmed's apartment building from the opposite direction. . . . Both cars contained only white officers; both were in plain view of Ahmed's home. . . . Rightly or wrongly, Ahmed regarded the obvious presence of the surveillance cars over several hours' time as threatening.

The report stressed that "against theories of an ambush or well-planned conspiracy stands the evidence that on Tuesday evening [July 23, 1968] Ahmed was annoyed and apprehensive about the police surveillance."

The Times experience, together with the report of the National Commission on the Causes and Prevention of Violence, strongly suggest that the assumption that the Cleveland disorder was planned is as yet unproved.

It may be significant that 14 out of the 19 police officials who expressed a view on the matter could find no evidence of planning in the disorders in their respective cities. In another instance, the police official said the disorder was planned, but he could offer no evidence in support of his statement. If this and the Cleveland case are added, the number of outbreaks that do not appear to have been planned comes to at least 16 out of 19.

In their assertions that police are now the principal targets of snipers, some observers give the impression that there have been large numbers of police casualties. In most cases, the reports have not been explicit in stating figures. However, as mentioned earlier, *U.S. News & World Report* cited 8 police deaths and 47 police woundings this past summer. In order to assess these reports, we obtained from police officials a breakdown of police casualties as a result of gunfire.

What we learned was that a total of four policemen were killed and that each death was by gunfire. But three of these occurred in one city, Cleveland; the other was in Inkster, Michigan. In other words, in 23 out of 25 cases where sniping was originally reported, no policemen were killed.

Our total agreed with figures initially taken from local press reports. However, our count of four dead was only half the figure reported in *U.S. News & World Report*. We learned why when we found that the story appearing in that magazine originally came from an Associated Press "roundup," which said that eight policemen had been killed by gunfire since July 1, 1968. But four of these eight cases were in the nature of individual acts of purely criminal—and not racial—violence. On July 2, a Washington, D.C., policeman was killed when he tried to arrest a man on a robbery complaint. A Philadelphia policeman was killed July 15 while investigating a $59 streetcar robbery. On August 5, in San Antonio, a policeman was killed by a 14-year-old boy he had arrested. The youth was a Mexican-American who had been arrested on a drinking charge. And, in Detroit, a policeman was shot to death on August 5 following a domestic quarrel. The circumstances concerning these four cases in no way display the features of a "new pattern" of violence.

The question of how many police *injuries* came from sniper fire is more complicated. A total of 92 policemen were injured, accounting for 14 out of 25 cases. Almost half the injuries—44—came from gunfire. In some instances, our findings showed a downward revision of our earlier information. In Gary, for example, somebody reportedly took a shot at Police Chief James F. Hilton as he cruised the troubled area shortly after the disturbance began. However, when interviewed, Chief Hilton vigorously denied the earlier report. In Peoria, 11 police officers were reportedly injured by shotgun blasts. However, Bernard J. Kennedy, Director of Public Safety, indicated that initial reports "were highly exaggerated" and that only seven officers were actually wounded. In East Point, Georgia, a white policeman had reportedly been injured during the disorder. Yet Acting Police Chief Hugh D. Brown indicated that there were no injuries to the police. In Little Rock, a policeman swore that he had been shot by a sniper. However, Chief of Police R. E. Brians told us that there was no injury and no broken skin. The Chief added that the policeman had been new and was not of the highest caliber. In fact, he is no longer with the department.

In addition, a closer look at the data reveals that the highest figures for numbers of policemen wounded by gunfire are misleading and need to be placed in perspective. Let us examine the three cases with the highest number of injuries: Cleveland with 10 policemen wounded by gunfire; Peoria, with seven; and Harvey-Dixmoor, Illinois, also with seven.

In Peoria, all seven policemen were wounded by the pellets from *a single shotgun blast.* In an interview, Safety

Director Kennedy stressed that "none of the injuries incurred were serious." The Harvey-Dixmoor incident was similar. There, five out of the seven injured were also hit by a single shotgun blast. Chief of Police Leroy H. Knapp Jr. informed us that only two or three shots were fired during the entire disorder. (A similar scattering of pellets occurred in St. Paul, where three out of four policemen hit by gunfire received their injuries from one shotgun blast.)

In Cleveland, almost every injury to a policeman came as a result of gunfire. However, it is not at all clear whether snipers inflicted the damage. In the chaos that accompanies many disorders, shots have sometimes been fired accidentally—by both rioters and policemen. Ripley's September 2 article in *The New York Times* stated the problem very well: "Only by setting the exact position of each man when he was shot, tracing the bullet paths, and locating all other policemen at the scene can a reasonable answer be found." Thus far, no information concerning the circumstances of each casualty in the Cleveland disorder has been disclosed, and this goes for deaths as well as injuries.

Moreover, what applies to Cleveland applies to the other disorders as well. The Little Rock case illustrates the point. Chief of Police Brians verified the shooting of a National Guardsman. However, he also clarified the circumstances of the shooting. He said that during the disorder a group of people gathered on a patio above a courtyard near the area where the National Guard was stationed. One individual, under the influence of alcohol, fired indiscriminantly into the crowd, hitting a guardsman in the foot. Chief Brians added: "He might just as easily have hit a [civil-rights] protestor as a guardsman." What is clear is that the circumstances concerning all casualties need to be clarified so as to avoid faulty inferences and incorrect judgments as much as possible.

Concerning the amount of sniping, there were numerous discrepancies between early and later reports, suggesting that many initial reports were exaggerated.

According to the police officials themselves, other than in the case of Cleveland where 25 to 30 snipers were allegedly involved, there were relatively few snipers. In 15 out of 17 cases where such information was available, police officials said there were three snipers or less. And in 7 out of 17 cases, the officials directly contradicted press reports at the time and said that no snipers were involved!

As for the number of gunshots fired by snipers, the reality, as reported by police, was again a lot less exciting than the newspapers indicated. In 15 out of 18 cases where information was available, "snipers" fired fewer than 10 shots. In 12 out of 18 cases, snipers fired fewer than five. Generally, then, in more than one-quarter of the cases in which sniping was originally reported, later indications were that no sniping had actually occurred.

In Evansville, initial reports indicated that a minimum of eight shots were fired. Yet Assistant Chief of Police Charles M. Gash told us that only one shot was fired.

A more dramatic illustration is found in the case of East Point, Georgia. Although 50 shots were reportedly fired at the time, Acting Chief of Police Hugh Brown informed us that no shots were fired.

In York, 11 persons were wounded in a "gun battle" on the first night. However, it turns out that 10 out of 11 persons were civilians and were injured by shotgun pellets. Only two snipers were involved, and only two to four shots were fired throughout the entire disturbance.

In Waterloo, Iowa, Chief of Police Robert S. Wright acknowledged that shots were fired, but he added: "We wouldn't consider it sniper fire." He told us that there was "no ambush, no concealment of participants, or anything like that." Moreover, he stated that not more than three persons out of a crowd of 50 youths carried weapons and "not a great number of shots were fired." The weapons used were small handguns.

In St. Paul, where 10 shots were reportedly fired at police and four officers were wounded by gunshots, Chief of Police Lester McAuliffe also acknowledged that though there was gunfire, there "wasn't any sniper fire as such."

A similar situation was found in Peoria. Safety Director Kennedy said that the three shots believed fired did not constitute actual sniping.

In Little Rock, Chief Brians discounted reports of widespread sniping and indicated that many "shots" were really firecrackers.

In Gary, early reports were that Chief of Police James Hilton had been fired upon and six persons had been wounded by snipers. Assistant Chief of Police Charles Boone told us that while a few shots might have been "fired in the air," no actual sniping occurred. No one was shot during the disturbance, and no one was injured. Chief Hilton indicated that the fireman who was supposed to have been hit during the outbreak was actually shot by a drunk *prior* to the disorder.

In a few instances, discrepancies between first reports and sober reappraisal can be traced to exaggerations of the policemen themselves. However, most of the discrepancies already cited throughout this report can be attributed to the press—at both the local and national level. In some instances, the early press reports (those appearing at the time of the incident) were so inexplicit as to give the *impression* of a great deal of sniping. In other instances, the early figures given were simply exaggerated. In still other instances, the early reports failed to distinguish between sniper fire and other forms of gunplay.

Moreover, the press generally gave far too little attention to the immediate cause or causes of the disturbance. Even in the aftermath of the violence, few attempts were made to verify previous statements or to survey the tensions and grievances rooted in the community. Instead, newspapers in many instances placed an unusually heavy (and at times distorted) emphasis on the most dramatic aspects of the violence, particularly where sniping was concerned.

A look at some of the newspaper headlines during the disorders is most revealing, especially where the "pellet cases" are involved. As mentioned earlier, large numbers of casualties were sustained from the pellets of a single shotgun blast—in Peoria, seven policemen; in Harvey-Dixmoor, five policemen, and in York, 10 civilians were injured in this way; the most commonly cited examples of a "new pattern" of violence. Unfortunately, inaccurate and sensational headlines created an impression of widespread sniping, with the police singled out as the principal targets. A few individual acts of violence were so enlarged as to convey to the reader a series of "bloodbaths." In some cases, an explanation of the circumstances surrounding the injuries was buried in the news story. In other cases, no explanation was given. In still other cases, the number of casualties was exaggerated.

Distorted headlines were found in the local press:

RACE VIOLENCE ERUPTS: DOZEN SHOT IN PEORIA
Chicago (Ill.) *Tribune,*
July 31, 1968

6 COPS ARE SHOT IN HARVEY STRIFE
Chicago *Sun-Times,*
August 7, 1968

20 HURT AS NEW VIOLENCE RAKES WEST END AREA
11 FELLED BY GUN FIRE, FOUR FIREMEN INJURED FIGHTING FIVE
BLAZES

York (Pa.) *Dispatch,*
August 5, 1968

These distortions were transmitted on the wire services as
well. For example, in Ann Arbor, Michigan, readers were
given the following accounts of Peoria and Harvey-Dixmoor
in their local newspapers. The first account was based upon a United Press International news dispatch; the second
is from an Associated Press dispatch.

10 POLICEMEN SHOT IN PEORIA VIOLENCE

By United Press International
Ann Arbor (Mich.) *News,*
July 30, 1968

Ten policemen were wounded by shotgun blasts today during a
four-hour flareup of violence in Peoria, Ill. . . .

EIGHT WOUNDED IN CHICAGO AREA

Ann Arbor *News,*
August 7, 1968

Harvey, Ill. (AP)—Sporadic gunfire wounded seven policemen
and a woman during a disturbance caused by Negro youths, and
scores of law enforcement officers moved in early today to secure
the troubled area. . . .

Finally, they were repeated in headlines and stories
appearing in the national press:

GUNFIRE HITS 11 POLICEMEN IN ILL. VIOLENCE

Washington Post,
July 31, 1968

SHOTGUN ASSAULTS IN PEORIA GHETTO WOUND
9 POLICEMEN

The Law Officer,
Fall, 1968

Chicago—On August 6, in the suburbs of Harvey and Dixmoor,
seven policemen and a woman were shot in Negro disturbances
which a Cook County undersheriff said bore signs of having been
planned.

U.S. News & World Report
August 19, 1968

In all probability, few newspapers or reporters could
withstand this type of criticism. Nevertheless, it does seem
that the national press bears a special responsibility. Few

of the nationally known newspapers and magazines attempted to verify sniping reports coming out of the cities; few were willing to undertake independent investigations of their own; and far too many were overly zealous in their reports of a "trend" based on limited and unconfirmed evidence. Stated very simply: The national press overreacted.

For some time now, many observers (including members of the academic community) have been predicting a change from spontaneous to premeditated outbreaks resembling guerrilla warfare. Their predictions have largely been based upon limited evidence such as unconfirmed reports of arms caches and the defiant, sometimes revolutionary rhetoric of militants.

And then came Cleveland. At the time, the July disorder in that city appeared to fulfill all the predictions—intelligence reports of planning prior to the disorder, intensive sniping directed at the police, the absence of a precipitating incident, and so on. Few people at the time quarreled with the appraisal in *The New York Times* that Cleveland was "perhaps the first documented case" of a planned uprising against the police. Following the events in Cleveland, disorders in which shots may have been fired were immediately suspected to be part of a "wave."

Unwittingly or not, the press has been constructing a scenario on armed uprisings. The story line of this scenario is not totally removed from reality. There *have* been a few shoot-outs with the police, and a handful may have been planned. But no wave of uprisings and no set pattern of murderous conflict have developed—at least not yet. Has the press provided the script for future conspiracies? Why hasn't the scenario been acted out until now? The answers to these questions are by no means certain. What is clear is that the press has critical responsibilities in this area, for any act of violence easily attracts the attention of the vicarious viewer as well as the participant.

Moreover, in an era when most Americans are informed by radio and television, the press should place far greater emphasis on interpreting, rather than merely reporting, the news. Background pieces on the precipitating events and tension-heightening incidents, more detailed information on the sniper himself, and investigations concerning police and civilian casualties represent fertile areas for the news analyst. To close, here is one concrete example: While four policemen were killed in the violence reviewed in this article, at least 16 civilians were also killed. A report on the circumstances of these deaths might provide some important insights into the disorders.

July/August 1969

FURTHER READING SUGGESTED BY THE AUTHOR:

The Paranoid Style in American Politics and Other Essays by Richard Hofstadter (New York: Knopf, 1966). A historian looks at the receptiveness of Americans to conspiratorial theories.

Shoot-out in Cleveland; Black Militants and the Police: July 23, 1968. A report of the Civil Violence Research Center by Louis H. Masotti and James J. Corsi (Cleveland, Ohio: Case Western Reserve University, submitted to the National Commission on the Causes and Prevention of Violence, May 16, 1969). This is an in-depth account of the background, nature, and circumstances of the July, 1968 disorder.

Public Information and Civil Disorders, National League of Cities, Department of Urban Studies (Washington, D.C.: July, 1968) contains recommendations concerning the activities of the news media during civil disorders.

Report of the National Advisory Commission on Civil Disorders (Washington, D.C.: Government Publishing Office, 1968). Chapter 15 evaluates the media coverage of civil disorders during the Summer of 1967.

Riot Commission Politics

MICHAEL LIPSKY/DAVID J. OLSON

Speaking before the National Commission on Civil Disorders, better known as the Kerner Commission, Kenneth Clark wondered aloud about the usefulness of what the commissioners and their staff were doing. There had been previous riot commissions, Clark reminded his audience, and they too had issued reports. But the whole undertaking had, for him, an Alice-in-Wonderland quality about it, "with the same moving picture reshown over and over again, the same analysis, the same recommendations, and the same inaction."

Kenneth Clark's skepticism is widely shared. But should we despair with him that riot commission reports are irrelevant? Or should we agree with public officials that riot commissions provide an invaluable service for helping society understand complex events? Or should we think cynically that riot commissions are no more than the tools by which chief executives placate and arouse people? These questions may only be answered by examining the place and function of riot commissions in the political life of the country. What do they really do? And how do they do it? How does one account for the great differences between expectations and results in the lives of recent riot commissions?

These questions open wide areas of disagreement, of course. But generally speaking, riot commissions are usually described in one or more of the following terms:

1. Government officials, it is sometimes thought, create riot commissions to provide authoritative answers to social and economic questions posed by riots, and to provide authoritative recommendations for preventing them in the future. This is certainly what commissions are *supposed* to do, as can be gleaned from reading the formal "charge" to any recent riot commission.

2. Others feel that riot commissions are simply a convenient way for public officials to buy time in which to formulate public policy. A harsher variant of this viewpoint has public officials creating commissions in a deliberate effort to evade political pressures and avoid coming to grips with the problem. A more sophisticated variant has the officials buying time so as not to have to deal with the passions *of the moment.* In the immediate aftermath of a riot, political executives have to conclude that neither the intense anger of blacks nor the intense fear and anger of whites are appropriate pressures or reliable indicators of what they should do.

3. It is said, also, that riot commissions are simply created to exonerate public officials from responsibility for the situation leading to the riot or for their behavior during it. In the recent past a number of commentators have inferred that riot commissions have "whitewashed" public officials.

4. Independent of the validity of the above three positions, it is said that riot commissions are irrelevant to the
political process. Essentially this seems to have been the
position of Kenneth Clark in his influential commission
testimony.

5. Regardless of the reasons for initiating riot commission activity in the first place, it may be said that riot commissions essentially function as interest groups, competing
with other interest groups in attempting to influence the
political environment in ways favorable to their general
orientations.

In recent research on the National Commission on Civil
Disorders (Kerner Commission), the Governor's Select
Commission on Civil Disorder of the State of New Jersey
(New Jersey Commission), and post-riot politics in Newark, Detroit and Milwaukee, we have tried to develop a
framework for analyzing some of the above considerations.
We conclude that formation of riot commissions gives rise
to public expectations which cannot be fulfilled and that
riot commissions are charged with incompatible goals
which cannot meaningfully be reconciled.

Insofar as this is the case, riot commissions are most
profitably viewed as participants in the ongoing political
struggle of American race relations. They may make marginal contributions to that struggle by providing status and
support for interpretations of riots which may affect the
decisions of other political actors. They may also provide
information about riots that will influence others, and may
lend legitimacy to information which is already available.
Riot commissions further may help structure the terms in
which debate over issues relating to riots will be pursued.
They are initiated by public officials as part of the executive
function, but they are transformed by their constituents

and, by virtue of the involvement of commissioners in commission business, they transform themselves into pressure group competitors in the political process.

But before discussing these points it will be useful to review some critical aspects of the Kerner Commission's operations. We will also mention related developments taking place in the New Jersey Commission where appropriate.

First, like other authoritative commissions appointed in recent times, the Kerner Commission was comprised of essentially conservative men. Of the eleven members named by President Lyndon B. Johnson on July 27, 1967, six were elected public officials, the most liberal of whom was Mayor John Lindsay (Republican) of New York City. Governor Otto Kerner, the chairman, was an Illinois Democrat known for his championing of both civil rights legislation and riot control training. Only two Negroes were named to the Commission, Senator Edward Brooke and Roy Wilkins, the most "respectable" of civil-rights leaders. The other members included Chief Herbert Jenkins of Atlanta, who enjoys a reputation for being a progressive among police chiefs; Katherine Peden, who was at the time Kentucky Commissioner of Commerce; and representatives of labor and business: I. W. Abel, President of the United Steel Workers, and Charles B. Thornton of Litton Industries. All of these people are either public officials or the heads of established American institutions. Indeed, as Tom Wicker wrote in his introduction to the Bantam edition of the Kerner Report, "President Johnson in appointing his Commission on Civil Disorders . . . was severely criticized for its moderate character." The McCone Commission, appointed by Governor Pat Brown of California following the Watts riot, and the New Jersey Commission were also made up of reputedly conservative people.

Second, the Kerner Commission began its work amidst conflicting pressures for action. As *The Washington Post* reported, the establishment of the Kerner Commission "followed several days of congressional demands for an investigatory group either from Congress or the White House. Johnson was under pressure to act before conservative opponents in Congress created their own commission." It was quite clear that the thrust of these investigations would be toward discovery of "conspiracies" and techniques of riot suppression.

Third, the research strategy of the Kerner Commission was highly complex and difficult to implement. The President charged it with a number of independent and delicate tasks. The first was to describe accurately what happened in each riot city, and to do it despite an extraordinary diversity of testimony. Adequate handling of this task alone would have had severe political implications. The finding of a conspiracy, for example, would support those skeptics of recent black political developments who would like to discount reports of widespread discontent among black people in American cities. A finding that no conspiracy existed, on the other hand, would lead analysis into the tangled network of social causation in racial matters about which there is great controversy. The President also asked the commission to explain why riots took place in some cities but not in others, even though previous studies on this question had proved to be singularly unsuccessful. Finally the President requested proposals on how to prevent future riots. This may have been the most politically perilous charge of all. It demanded a review and evaluation of reform planning that would have to be convincing to (first) the commissioners and (then) the public. The peril lies in the fact that such a task raises questions of the capacity of this system to respond to social needs and the adequacy of previous programs. This diffuse research agenda had to be accomplished *in less than a year.*

1. *The Scarcity of Time and Resources.* Such tight schedules are not peculiar to riot commissions, but the Kerner Commission and other recent riot commissions seem particularly hampered by these constraints. It is uncertain whether any riot commission could adequately fulfill the research goals with which they are charged. Almost as soon as commissions are convened, their directors find themselves confronted by critical deadlines. They must hire staff quickly without the luxury of fully assessing their qualifications and before the research agenda has even been completed. One consequence is that generalists, such as lawyers, may be hired over specialists, since staff directors may not know precisely what they want to do. The Kerner Commission was especially hampered because in late August talented people in the academic world were already committed, and because hiring had to proceed in the face of widespread skepticism such as that expressed by Kenneth Clark.

As soon as staff is hired, the pressure is on to collect the data. Investigation must follow quickly upon the occurrence of riots because of the need to interview witnesses while memories are still fresh and because proposed solutions presumably depend upon a research effort. The Kerner Commission decided to obtain information on riots in 20 cities, including environmental background features and interviews with key people, from city officials to militant civil-rights activists. The data-gathering teams went into the field at a time when December 15 was considered the target date for an "interim" report. This meant they had about two months in which to uncover the facts about the

riots, the cities in which they occurred, and possible explanations for their occurrence. Obviously, this was too
short a time period to obtain sufficient data to develop
well-rounded studies, a fact confirmed by the Kerner Commission's decision not to develop all of these profiles for
publication. The New Jersey Commission, given less than
three months to hire staff and conduct and assemble research, was similarly constrained by time.

Another consequence of having to produce reports under
this kind of pressure is that the staff is almost obliged to
develop (or simply accept) a general working theory of riot
causation to guide the research. The outlines of the theory
are familiar to anyone who has looked into almost any recent commission report. It holds that systematic deprivation
and discrimination in the past, when added to reasonable
expectations of positive change and when accompanied by
continued indignities and community resentments, become
focused by a single incident or series of incidents into behavior that takes the form of looting and other hostile activities. As a general theory this is perfectly serviceable, but
it hardly accounts for the varieties of civil disorders, which
Presidents, governors, and others are concerned about. Social scientists, especially, must find this unsatisfactory, since
they are interested in explaining variation, rather than explaining why something does or does not exist. The questions of why riots occurred in some cities and not in others,
or why riots varied in form and intensity, can be sensibly
addressed only through a more rigorous comparative analysis than there was time to undertake in the work of recent
riot commissions. Farming out research to social scientists
was one way the Kerner Commission attempted to deal
with research difficulties, but this was not entirely satis-
factory.

As individuals with public constituencies, commissioners

have to be assured that their decisions rest upon irrefutable and unambiguous evidence. The time problem intrudes when commission staffs anticipate these needs and try to "build a case," an effort that detracts in some ways from an open research strategy and diverts staff members from other duties. Staffers on the Kerner Commission, for example, had to return to the field to obtain affidavits from witnesses on whose testimony the narrative summaries of disorders rested. Staff investigators of the New Jersey Commission were required to file individual memoranda on every person with whom they talked on commission business. "Building a case" and good research procedures are not necessarily incompatible. But a strain is placed upon mutual satisfaction of both these goals when time is short. Statistics without relevance are collected; time-consuming procedures are honored to make an impression of thoroughness; theories with potential validity are rejected since they cannot be adequately tested, and so on.

Related to the demands for building a case is what happens when commissions begin to focus attention on the single task of producing the final document. At this point, other talents, perhaps antithetical to those of the researcher, are demanded of the staff. These are the ability to work all day and night, the capacity to absorb endless criticism without taking personal affront, and the ability to synthesize the sentiments of the commissioners, or to anticipate their sentiments regarding various issues. These qualities are those of lawyers, of advocates who work under pressure for clients regardless of personal interests or allegiance to material. In this respect commission staff-domination by lawyers may be a necessary rather than an accidentally perverse quality of commissions. But the point remains that those best able to gather and interpret socially relevant data may not perform well in accommodating to the pressures that are brought to bear in writing the final report.

The pressures of time are also incompatible with a rational search for answers. Under rational procedures, study should be followed by conclusions, followed by program suggestions relating to those conclusions. But lack of time required recent riot commissions to formulate their programs at the same time as they were analyzing causes. This is not to say that their conclusions do not follow from the analysis. But this dynamic helps explain why there need not be a relationship between the factual analysis of events and commissions' proposals for change.

Scarcity of resources also contributes to the typical shakiness of the organization of riot commissions. Commissions enjoy no regular budgetary status, nor do they continue to enjoy top executive priority after their creation has served to reassure the executive's constituency that he has acted on the problem. The Kerner Commission, for example, was originally promised sufficient funds to accomplish their task, but it was later discouraged from seeking more money because in late 1967 it had become presidential policy to seek no supplementary appropriations from Congress, and because federal agencies were reluctant to contribute to the commission from their diminished budgets.

2. *Developing Commission Integration.* It is the peculiar dilemma of riot commissions that commissioners are apparently chosen for the diversity of interests they represent, while at the same time they are expected to agree on, and support, a meaningful report about a complex problem with clear ideological overtones. This circumstance sometimes leads the public to assume, quite understandably, that the final report of any given commission will be little

more than a collection of bland generalities, or an out-and-out whitewash. If it is the first, it will be because the commissioners were in fact representative of diverse and conflicting interests and were unable to agree on anything controversial. And if it is the second, it will be because they were really chosen by the political leadership for the basic congruence of their views. Either way, the appointment of riot commissions has led to rather unflattering expectations of their work, and often justifiably so, given the extent to which recent commissions have been made up of incumbent or former public officials and bona fide members of high-status organizations such as trade unions, financial conglomerates, or the press.

Riot commissions are made up of men chosen for diversity of interests, and they are inherently temporary. Thus riot commissions are confronted in extraordinary fashion with the problems inherent in all complex organizations —the development of mechanisms of socialization and the development of group norms and values which may overcome tendencies toward fragmentation and disintegration. In practical terms, tendencies toward fragmentation and disintegration in riot commissions may take the forms of developing minority reports and developing destructive tensions between commissioners and staff.

For some commissioners, a minority report represents a threat with which, within limits, they can manipulate other commissioners to modify their views. The strong language of the summary of the Kerner Commission Report, for example, can be attributed to Mayor Lindsay and his staff, who in the weeks just prior to the final approval of the report had come to feel that the commission's approach was not sufficiently hard-hitting. Lindsay seized on the fact that a draft of the summary had not yet been prepared and had his staff develop one. He presented it to the commission as a statement of his position, indicating (it is not clear how explicitly) that he would issue such a statement anyway, if the commission failed to support him. The other commissioners, recognizing that the "summary" prepared by Lindsay reflected the report's contents, and that Lindsay might well release the summary in some form anyway, adopted it as their own. Mayor Lindsay's outspoken comments on the needs of cities may have had the effect of moving some commissioners toward his views in order to keep him in the fold. In any event, it is safe to conclude that the Kerner Commission summary would not have been so dramatic a document if Lindsay had not forced the issue in this way.

But, in a sense, a minority report is an ultimate weapon. One must still account for how commissioners with diverse interests and viewpoints come to identify themselves with the final product of a commission. Under what circumstances do such men permit themselves the luxury of political compromise in endorsing views to which they may not totally subscribe?

One way to explain the surprisingly provocative quality of both the Kerner Commission and the New Jersey Commission reports, given the essentially conservative cast of their members, is that their staff directors explicitly encouraged and engineered the development of *a sense of urgency* within these commissions. Direct exposure to ghetto conditions was perhaps the most successful technique to this end. Members of the Kerner Commission conducted two-day tours of riot areas, sometimes even without the company of the press corps or the guiding hands of city officials. One of the most successful of these took place in Cincinnati on August 30 when Mayor Lindsay and Senator Fred Harris, two of the most liberal members of the commission, met alone with a group of black nationalists. They were frankly informed of the group's dedication to the destruction of American society as now constituted. The confrontation apparently was particularly meaningful for Lindsay and Harris because the nationalists were highly educated men, and so could not be dismissed as being merely frustrated because of restricted mobility.

By the same token, the New Jersey Commission staff arranged for their commissioners to divide into teams of two and accompany antipoverty workers into Newark ghetto homes, bars, and barber shops. Most participants, including chairman Robert Lilley, credited these tours with creating the sense of awareness and alarm about ghetto conditions that was ultimately reflected in the final report.

This facet of commission procedure in part was born of political necessity. Staff research was not immediately available to the commissioners, yet they had to demonstrate to the public that they were doing *something*. One way to do this was to study conditions firsthand. Happily, this also permitted commissioners to learn about ghetto conditions and agree on the nature of ghetto existence before policy papers were prepared and before it became necessary to "take sides."

Exposure to formal witnesses with dramatic testimony was also useful in creating a sence of urgency. Kenneth Clark's appearance before the Kerner Commission was considered influential in offering perspective to the commissioners on their activity. The same effect was produced when the staffs of both the Kerner Commission and the New Jersey Commission circulated articles by Robert Blauner and by Robert Fogelson that were highly critical of the McCone Commission. These articles alerted everyone

to the potential public criticism of "wishy-washy" riot reports. Many New Jersey commissioners reported being
heavily influenced by the testimony of black shopkeepers
whose stores were shot up by New Jersey policemen; shopkeepers, after all, were not likely to be malcontents.

Problems of potential fragmentation threaten commission unity at all stages. Initially, the problem is one of
getting commissioners to think of themselves as *commissioners,* not as individual politicians. This is helped, as
we saw, by creating a sense of urgency among commission
members. In later stages, the problem becomes one of conflicts arising from the fact that commissioners must begin
to take stands on matters of public policy.

Considerable conflict did develop in the work of recent
commissions at the writing stages, but these conflicts did
not erupt to the extent that minority reports were filed or
that serious public displays of conflict emerged in the press.
The Kerner Commission did not break up over the ap-
propriateness of criticizing major social institutions or over
the ultimate tone and emphasis of the report summary, although these were issues of considerable conflict within
the commission. Neither did the New Jersey Commission
break up over the issue of recommending governmental
consolidation for Essex County, although the commission
was significantly divided over this issue. Commissioners
clearly preferred to accept compromise rather than diminish
the total impact of the report because of open conflict or
sniping at the document. Members of both commissions
have refrained from dissociating themselves from aspects of
the reports, and many have actively defended them, despite
the controversies they have set off.

Although there were considerable disagreements on the
various commissions, what is significant were the areas of

agreement. So far as we can discover there was little dispute over the causes of riots. The commissioners agreed that the riots were not results of conspiracies nor mass behavior dominated by criminal or quasi-criminal elements. Rather, these men (and one woman) chosen for their community standing and their connection with established institutions —people, in other words, who were relatively conservative in the literal sense—attributed the riots to long-standing factors of discrimination, deprivation, and neglect. They condemned violence and criminal behavior, but they recognized that riots could be understood as products of central tendencies in American life.

There was also no question that extraordinary measures would have to be taken if the country wanted to deal seriously with the social bases of urban unrest. What debate there was concerned the kinds of measures that would have to be undertaken, and the kinds of criticism of American institutions appropriate for public discussion. But on the whole, these disagreements over the nature of the recommendations are less significant than the commissioners' agreement on the necessity for radical departures from existing public policy. When viewed in the light of the political and social legitimacy commanded by recent riot commissions, this is the significance of recent commission reports.

Apart from the danger of conflict among the commissioners, there is also the possibility of conflict between them and their staffs. In this regard, an important point of tension is the commissioners' need to feel reassured that staff members are free from bias and are presenting their work free from ideological distortion. Commissioners' suspicions apparently focus upon two possibilities. On the one hand, some staff members are feared to be overzealous for social reform, with a corresponding bias emerging in their work.

This possibility is somewhat reinforced by the nature of lower-level staff recruitment, where an interest in social reform may be significant in the type of person willing to work for commissions on short notice. The field staff of the Kerner Commission, for example, was made up to a significant degree of young lawyers and returned Peace Corp volunteers. On the other hand, formally bipartisan commissions encounter suspicion that top staff members are really very partisan and have been selected to whitewash elected officials.

The dangers of failure to allay commission suspicions that the staff is overzealous or partisan are two: The commissioners may reject staff work and in the end develop conclusions independent of staff analysis; or, in anticipation of commission antagonism, staff work may be screened to provide commissioners with only "acceptable" material. In either case, the commission runs the risk of staff revolt, the erosion of organizational loyalty among the staff, and divisive public debate inspired by discontented staff.

The Kerner Commission was confronted with all these difficulties. The issue of staff political partisanship arose because some staff members were considered to have developed significant personal stakes in an "Administration outcome" for the final report, and the selection of David Ginsburg as the commission's Executive Director did little to allay concern that the Executive Director would be fronting for the President. Ginsburg is a partner in one of Washington's biggest law firms, has extensive government connections, and was known to participate in White House social circles.

Openness and responsiveness of staff procedures, and symbolic staff appointments, are two strategies available to commission staffs in allaying commissioner fears of partisanship. The staff directors of the Kerner Commission and the New Jersey Commission spent a great deal of energy consulting with commission members about ways in which they wanted to proceed. David Ginsburg and Victor Palmieri, the Deputy Executive Director of the Kerner Commission, were distinctly aware of the possible dangers of commissioners' suspicions. Sanford Jaffe, Executive Director of the New Jersey Commission, also indicated that gaining the confidence of potentially suspicious commissioners was one of his major concerns. In the Kerner Commission, the deep involvement of John Lindsay's assistant, Jay Kriegel, in commission activities contributed to alleviating Republican concerns over a potential "whitewash." The same could be said of the high-level appointments of Richard Nathan and Stephen Kurzman, both of whom had worked for Republican congressmen. Although staff directors of the Kerner Commission insist that these men were not appointed for partisan reasons, their presence was considered by other staff members to have helped reduce fears of partisanship.

Ideological splits between commissioners and staff are more difficult to control and can be quite damaging to ultimate commission influence. The prestige of the McCone Commission, for example, was severely undermined by critics who argued that the conservative cast of the commission substantially ignored the findings of its social science staff and consultants. The writings of Robert Blauner, Robert Fogelson, Paul Jacobs, and Harry Scoble reflect this. During the life of the Kerner Commission, as well, major difficulties emerged over staff suspicions that their analyses were being rejected on conservative grounds.

The most obvious and best publicized example of this commissioner/staff tension revolved around the rejection of a document entitled, "The Harvest of American Racism" drafted by social scientists employed by the Kerner

Commission. From all indications, it appears that this draft was rejected for inclusion in the final report not only because its conclusions were radical, but also because documentation for its underlying theory of riot causation was lacking. There was also a problem of communication within the commission. The social scientists were shocked to find the document that they considered only a draft treated as a final product. This was devastating because the social scientists assumed it was clear that adequate documentation had not yet been appended to the theoretical analysis. On the other hand, the chief staff directors of the commission were no less dismayed to receive what they considered an unsubstantiated theoretical piece. The staff directors argued that for commissioners to accept a provocative analysis required, at the very least, that it be grounded in a solid evidential base.

Very shortly after the "Harvest" draft was rejected, the commission changed its timetable to eliminate the interim report and released most of the staff, about 100 people. For some staff members, these three events confirmed their suspicions that the commission was exploiting them without respect for their skills and was leaning toward development of a conservative report that was at odds with the staff members' analysis. Leaks to the press followed, and at least one commission consultant held a press conference to discuss these matters publicly. Thus, for a period in the latter half of December the Kerner Commission was under considerable pressure in the press to deny charges that it was heading in a conservative direction.

Release of the final report allayed these fears. Previously critical staff members now acknowledge this and, indeed, that much of their analysis was woven into the final document. By taking their fears to the press, these staff members may have contributed to the outcome by putting pressure on the commission at a critical time.

3. *The Development of Political Legitimacy.* Initially, riot commissions are charged with generating objective analysis and impartial recommendations based upon this analysis. Initially, commissioners are recruited because of their status, their imputed objectivity and responsibility, and the extent to which they appear to be representative of a spectrum of diverse interests. We have suggested, however, that if commission efforts are to be successful, commissioners must give up some of their self and occupational role interests and develop orientations toward the commission as an organization with a life of its own. As this happens riot commissions adopt strategies to maximize the impact of the final report. We have already mentioned the example of staff directors formulating procedures to discourage minority reports. They recognize that a commission that appears to be substantially divided merely testifies to the complexity of the issue and is supportive of many viewpoints.

An insight into the efforts of riot commissions to develop legitimacy can be found in the tension between pursuit of a "scientific" research strategy (or "scientific" legitimacy) and the political needs of commission work (or "political" legitimacy). Staffs must conduct inquiries so that the commission appears comprehensive in searching for explanations and program proposals, reliable in presentation of evidence, and cognizant of advanced work in various research and program areas. This image must be secured by the staff for the commission whether or not information so obtained is related to questions or answers of commission interest.

Staff directors must conserve scarce time. Yet the staff directors of the Kerner Commission traveled throughout the country to demonstrate (as well as assure) that they had conferred with the broadest base of social scientists and were searching widely for expertise.

Moreover, mechanisms had to be developed to deal with numerous inquiries from people offering their services (for a fee) and research findings. These inquiries and proposals had to be handled in such a way as to give the impression that offers of help were indeed welcome (when in many cases they were not). In this regard the Kerner Commission confronted a problem endemic to most government agencies. But unlike most government agencies, the commission lacked a routine for dealing with these inquiries, the staff to handle them, or the time to evaluate them.

An illustration of this is the case of a prominent research-oriented psychiatrist who submitted his name through his Senator, Edward Brooke, a Kerner Commission member, for one of the top research positions on the commission. He did not receive a reply until some months after the commission was thoroughly staffed. Then he received a formula response, thanking him for his inquiry concerning a "job" at the commission, but explaining that positions were no longer available. The man was insulted, and was subsequently uncooperative with the commission. The peremptory posture assumed by top staff members of the Kerner Commission of necessity, given the strain under which they operated, was resented in many quarters—both in academic circles and in staffs of subnational commissions. Especially irksome to the Kerner Commission was the fact that from the outset there was general recognition of the time trial the commission would experience; thus the commission was "marked" for exploitation by individuals convinced they could help, or convinced that the commission could help them.

Besides establishing their "scientific" legitimacy, commissions must give the impression that all political groups are given their day in court. Sometimes the motives for hearing certain witnesses are transparently political rather than educational or evidential. The Kerner Commission, for example, took the testimony of many of the black militants whose names appear on the witness list at a period when many chapters in the report already had been approved in relatively final form.

So far, we have been building an argument that the internal political dynamics of riot commissions can be characterized as the gradual development of *a pressure group*. This is particularly curious because, in the first place, riot commissions are established by public officials as objective instrumentalities to provide authoritative answers to questions of concern (thus, they are *government* organizations) ; and, in the second place, because riot commissions are specifically designed for the representation of *diverse* interests when originally formed.

Nevertheless, this view of riot commissions as developing into pressure groups may help explain both their strengths and weaknesses. Insofar as a diverse group of implicitly responsible, high status individuals subscribe to one interpretation of civil disorders and subscribe to a single set of recommendations, riot commissions may claim a high degree of political legitimacy. This is their strength. But insofar as a riot commission must compete in the political arena without being able to rely upon the organizational status of individual commission members, riot commissions enter an ideological arena where they must compete with other groups in the political process. In that competition, the impact of commissions is predictably marginal. The executive who creates a riot commission assigns to it the function of authoritatively articulating goals for the alleviation of problems of civil disorders. But the goals become authoritative for the larger political system only insofar as they are accepted by other groups for conversion into public policy. In the absence of such acceptance, the recommendations remain only as political demands. They are purely recommendatory or advisory unless supportive relations can be established with interest groups and other key actors.

In attempting to develop political coalitions and influence the political process, riot commissions adopt a variety of strategies to overcome their relatively powerless status. These strategies include: (1) maximizing the visibility and controlling the exposure of the reports; (2) competing for legitimacy; (3) affecting the political environment; and (4) assisting the implementation process.

1. *Maximizing Visibility.* Riot commissions are concerned with creating favorable images of their activities, and attempt to do so by giving maximum visibility to their reports. The tone adopted in the reports reflects this concern. Both the Kerner Commission and the New Jersey Commission elected to develop what appear to be hard-hitting documents. In the Kerner Commission Report, as everyone recalls, "white racism" was identified as the overriding primal cause of conditions leading to riots. This was sensational, assuring a maximum impact for the commission's labors. At the same time, however, the commission report contained almost no criticism of established institutions or programs. Criticism of national-level programs is largely lacking—despite the fact that the federal government is the only locus for the kind of effort that is called for in the report—and criticism is minimized of trade unions, big-city mayors, and other groups who might be expected to do something about the alleged "racism."

The tone achieved by this report was not arrived at accidentally, according to a number of high-level staff members. The commission explicitly decided to produce a moral statement on the evils of racism and implicitly agreed not to specify the institutions perpetuating the condemned racism. Clearly the day-to-day interpersonal brand of racial hostility was not what the Kerner Commission had most in mind when it condemned white racism. The only way that white racism makes sense as a root cause of civil disorders is in terms of its location in and legacy for major American institutions.

The commission apparently avoided criticizing these institutions partly because to do so might destroy the commission's unity (those very institutions being represented on the Kerner Commission in the persons of business leader Thornton, Police Chief Jenkins, labor leader Abel), partly because to criticize these institutions would have involved the commission in nationwide debates with powerful organizations intent on defending themselves, and partly because the commission was dependent upon these institutions to put into effect their recommendations. Thus, criticism of past performances were apparently avoided in the hope that future positive commitments might be forthcoming.

When it comes to manipulating the terms in which commission reports will be received and evaluated, the powers of commissions are extremely limited. The phrase "white racism," for example, which appears but once in the summary of the report, captured the focus of the press to a greater extent than any other single finding reported by the Kerner Commission. From a rereading of the summary, however, it would appear that the commission had hoped that national attention would center on the conclusion that the country was "moving toward two societies, one black, one white—separate and unequal." Similarly, the New Jersey Commission felt obligated to address the issue of official corruption in Newark because of repeated testimony on that subject by commission witnesses. On release of the report, the press, especially in Newark, gave a great deal of attention to the corruption issue, although it had a relatively minor place in the report itself. New Jersey Commission members indicated in interviews that they regretted including the corruption issue at all, because it tended to draw attention away from more important findings of their report.

2. *Competing for Legitimacy.* In attempting to influence other political actors on behalf of their report, riot commissions, as we have seen, try to establish firmly their claims as the authoritative interpreters of civil disorders and as authoritative planners for preventing future civil disorder. These claims do not go uncontested. Other groups have access to the same symbols and similar grounds of legitimacy.

Simply stated, one riot commission often begets another, or two or three. The competing riot commissions have less claim to objectivity or being "official," but they have greater claims to reliable constituencies and the group status that results. These constituencies are, for one reason or another, determined to undermine the monopoly of legitimacy asserted by the riot commissions and attempt to establish legitimacy of their own. They adopt the commission inquiry form in order to capitalize on the acceptability of this political instrument.

The political logic appears to be as follows: if it can be shown that opposite conclusions can emerge from the same kind of investigation of civil disorders, then it can be argued that the conclusion of the authoritative commission was the product of the biases of commissioners. This is all quite explicit, and antagonistic interest groups don't hesitate to use the tactic even when it is patently clear that the "competing commission" is undertaking a biased investigation. Take, for example, the remarks of John J. Heffernan, President of the New Jersey State Patrolmen's Benevolent Association, when he "predicted" the findings of his association's investigation: "We are appalled at the findings of the [New Jersey] riot commission, especially in the interests of law and order. The PBA riot study and investigation committee is certainly going to come up with different findings."

After President Johnson issued an executive order creating the Kerner Commission, the United States Senate authorized the Permanent Subcommittee on Investigations of the Committee on Government Operations (McClellan Committee) "to make a full and complete study and investigation of riots . . . and measures necessary for their immediate and long-range prevention." The McClellan Committee's investigations have attempted to undermine the findings of the Kerner Commission by centering on Office of Economic Opportunity personnel involved in riots, hearing witnesses who allege that there is a conspiracy behind the riots, and generally giving a hostile reception to other witnesses not sympathetic with the committee's more conservative views. That President Johnson himself tried to undermine his own Kerner Commission is perhaps not surprising. The fact that he included in his charge to the (Milton) Eisenhower Commission on the Causes and Prevention of Violence the duty to investigate civil disorders is consistent with his other acts of unsympathetic reception of the Kerner Report. The New Jersey Commission's "Report For Action," released in February of 1968, shortly thereafter triggered the New Jersey State Patrolmen's Benevolent Association's Riot Study Commission report entitled "A Challenge To Conscience." In Detroit, Jerome P. Cavanagh's Mayor's Development Team represented a public response to local civil disorders with most commission members drawn from city agencies and the Mayor's Office. But the Development Team was soon challenged by the New Detroit Committee, a private counter-thrust to the public commission. In California, the conservative McCone Commission was countered, both as to its findings and its recommendations, by the California Advisory Committee to the United States Commission on Civil Rights.

These competing commissions employ many of the same strategies and tactics as official riot commissions in manipu-ating the symbols of legitimacy. They follow closely the procedures of the initial commissions, including assembling a staff, holding formal hearings, conducting investigations, hearing witnesses, collecting documents, and offering rec-ommendations. In fact, they are often the same witnesses, the same documents, and similar investigations. But their findings and recommendations vary considerably from the conclusions of initial commissions. Riot commissions, whether initial or competing, thus represent ad hoc devices by which on-going antagonistic interests compete for po-litical legitimacy.

3. *Affecting the Political Environment.* In content, com-mission reports can be analyzed as attempts to reassure various publics in an otherwise unsettled environment. These reassurances may take the form of dispelling popular rumors and myths, or they may take the form of interpret-ing disturbing events in ways that can be absorbed within traditional American beliefs.

Efforts to reassure various publics begin as soon as com-missions are formed. Early testimony plays an important part in giving the appearance that significant interests are being represented. J. Edgar Hoover's statement that he had no evidence of a conspiracy was the only testimony released officially during the first set of Kerner Commission hearings. Then, as if to counteract the information that the chief criminal investigative official of the United States had no evidence of a riot conspiracy, Governor Kerner informed reporters that Sargent Shriver, Director of the Office of Economic Opportunity, and Robert Weaver, Secretary of Housing and Urban Development, both had evidence of the presence of unidentified strangers in neighborhoods shortly before riots broke out. In those days of crisis, it would appear that members of the Kerner Commission wanted to reassure the public that questions of law and order would receive high priority. But, recognizing that Hoover's testimony appeared to preclude a search for confirmation of a theory widely held by some Americans, Governor Kerner "scrambled" the first message in order to protect the commission from early criticism.

Beyond dispelling myths such as those of conspiracy, riot commissions also reaffirm traditionally accepted views of society. They uniformly condemn violence and reaffirm the principles of law and order. They also commonly invoke that series of beliefs in the American creed pertaining to "equality" and "integration." Note the concluding sentence to the Kerner Commission's chapter on the history of Negro protest: "Negro protest for the most part, has been firmly rooted in the basic values of American society, seeking not their destruction, but their fulfillment." Which values? Which America? The statement may have empirical validity when interpreted, but here it has primarily inspirational value.

Of course riot commissions cannot reassure everyone. Reassuring the black community that commissions are sensitive to their feelings about white racism risks arousing the anger of previously uninvolved white groups who violently object to this explanation of riots. Obviously this was the case with the Kerner Commission's focus on "white racism." The New Jersey Commission tried to reassure Newark blacks that their grievances had been heard and would be articulated in the commission report. But this intention was undermined by the controversial nature of its program recommendations. Half of the New Jersey commissioners argued that political consolidation of Essex County was the only means of establishing a tax base that would give Newark the resources to solve its problems. But other commissioners argued against consolidation on the grounds that this would, in effect, preclude the election of a Negro mayor precisely at the time when black people were becoming a majority of the city electorate. The first position risked disturbing white suburbanites upon whose support implementation of commission recommendations rested. The second argument risked reassuring Negroes of electoral success without providing the resources for basic services.

Riot commissions can attempt to quiet unreasonable fears, and reassure segments of the population that their needs are being addressed. But they cannot escape the difficulties that are incurred when controversal program recommendations are considered necessary. Recent commissions have explicitly chosen controversy at the expense of tranquility, but in doing so they have risked arousing political antagonists in the struggle over program recommendations.

These last remarks have been directed toward the more symbolic content of commission activity. More explicitly, riot commissions also attempt to affect the environment in which reports are received by treating gently the riot-related behavior of the executive, and by anticipating the needs of other political actors. Because of their relative powerlessness, commissions are dependent upon the favorable reception of their reports by the executive and other centers of power for maximum impact on the larger political system. However, these same political executives may have been involved in dealing with the control of the civil disorders and with programs related to the basic causes of the disorders. Thus the possibility is raised of commission's having to deal critically with the behavior of the political executives upon whom they are at least partially dependent for the implementation of their recommendations.

One drawback in exonerating the actions of the executive in civil disorders is that it gives credence to competing riot commissions in challenging the initial commission's claims to legitimacy. The New Jersey Commission strongly criticized the city administration in Newark. It left virtually untouched the matter of the Governor's actions at the time of the disorder, which were widely perceived by the black community in Newark to be inflammatory. During the Newark disturbances, Governor Hughes had told reporters that he would draw the line between the law and the jungle, and that riots were criminal and unrelated to civil-rights protests. Naturally enough, city officials in Newark lost no time in pointing out the discrepancy between the commission's statements about the Mayor of Newark and the Governor of New Jersey.

Riot commissions also attempt to further their recommendations by anticipating the needs of other important political actors. The Kerner Commission at one point adopted an end-of-the-year deadline for its interim report in part to obtain consideration in the formulation of the President's budget messages. Later it adopted the President's "message on the cities" as a framework for some of its programmatic recommendations, on the assumption that this would appear to coincide with his legislative goals and thus receive President Johnson's endorsement. The commission also consulted with cabinet officers before releasing its report. This strategy was based on the erroneous assumption that the President would use the commission's recommendations as a tool for furthering his own domestic program.

4. *Strategies for Implementation.* It is appropriate to conclude by mentioning a number of explicit strategies that riot commissions adopt to affect the reception of their product in the political arena. Riot commissions have recently advocated extending commission life in one form or another. The McCone Commission, for example, chose this means for advancing its recommendations. Near the end of the New Jersey Commission's deliberations, a request was made to Governor Richard Hughes to establish an ongoing review body including some members of the commission. A commissioner on Mayor Cavanagh's Development Team indicated that after the MDT issued its report, it was decided that an executive committee composed of the Mayor and five of the Mayor's top assistants should meet periodically to review what was happening to the MDT report.

The major drawback to this approach has been the lack of power of the commissions once reports are issued. If riot commissions themselves have relatively little power, then a few of the commission members meeting periodically have even less power in the implementation process. Paul Jacobs suggests that what the periodic review undertaken by the McCone Commission actually accomplished was "defending itself [the commission] against some of the attacks which have been made upon it," and serving a public-relations function. Governor Hughes never granted the request of the New Jersey Commission to be reconstituted as an ongoing review body. In Detroit, the Mayor's Development Team was able to continue meeting periodically, and since many of the members of the MDT were public officials, it was able to participate in the implementation process. The MDT illustrates another aspect to the commission paradox. Commissions comprised of public officials may indeed have power in the implementation process, but they will lack the reputation for objectivity on which their persuasive powers rest.

Commissioners as individuals have attempted to exert pressure on public officials for implementation. In New Jersey, for example, Governor Hughes was threatened by individual members of the commission with public criticism if he continued his failure to respond. Shortly thereafter, the Governor and his staff received members of the commission and in an all-day session virtually wrote the Governor's special message to the legislature. This message, which called for expenditures of $126.1 million on welfare, housing, education, law enforcement and urban problems, incorporated most of the commission's recommendations pertaining to New Jersey state government.

Let us now try to evaluate the assumptions about riot commissions that were identified at the beginning of this essay.

1. Riot commissions are inherently incapable of providing sophisticated answers to the most important questions relating to riots. As government agencies limited in time, resources, and staff, riot commissions can contract for a limited number of empirical studies, investigate the validity of some rumors and myths surrounding civil disorders, and make relatively intelligent judgments in describing riot oc-

currences. They can also make sound program proposals, though they must do so before critical research has been completed. Recommendations of riot commissions may be said to be authoritative in the sense that they are comprised of high-status individuals and are accorded high status by the fact that they were created by the chief executive. But their recommendations are authoritative only insofar as the chief executive moves to implement them.

To the extent that the chief executive fails to move toward implementation—as in the case of President Johnson—or to the extent that recommendations go beyond the scope of executive powers—as in the case of the New Jersey recommendations regarding Newark corruption—riot commissions must be seen not as authoritative but as competitive pressure groups in the political process. As such their influence is restricted to the legitimacy that they can capture and the political skills of individual commissioners who attempt to affect implementation.

2. It is rather fruitless to enter the murky area of the motivation of executives who create riot commissions. But our analysis does permit us to say a few things. Whether or not riot commissions are created in order to buy time, it is unquestionable that they do permit public officials to avoid immediate pressures for action and to postpone decisions for many months. Not only does the creation of a commission deflect pressures from the chief executive, but it also improves his bargaining position in a conservative direction by permitting him to claim that he is constrained by other political pressures over which he has little control. In the intense crisis following the riot, people seem to appeal instinctively to the chief executive for leadership. But the opportunity for decisive leadership, for making qualitatively different decisions about national priorities, based

on opportunities available only in crisis situations, may not be what the politician desires. Postponement permits the chief executive to wrap himself in the usual constraints of office where politics as usual will continue to obtain. Riot commissions also contribute to cooling of tensions by reassuring various publics in a symbolic way that their needs are being met. This may take the form of calling witnesses representative of various positions, making hortatorical appeals for justice and nonviolence, and so forth.

3. Is there something inherent in riot commissions that supports allegations that they are established to "whitewash" public officials? We may ask this apart from the question of whether some commissions are made up of members picked primarily for their unquestionable support of a chief executive. We think there is a built-in tendency toward the whitewash, to the extent that riot commissions minimize criticism of the public official to whom they must look for primary implementation of the report. Further, for the sake of commission solidarity and to avoid diminishing the report's impact by the airing of dissension, riot commissions minimize criticisms of institutions with which individual commissioners are intimately associated. To some extent, public officials attempt to influence commissions in favorable ways through appointments of political allies and "reliable" individuals to the commission. As we have suggested, however, this strategy will have limited returns because of the fears of partisan bias and the need to make the commission appear "representative."

4 and 5. Kenneth Clark's skepticism over the relevance of riot commissions is essentially justified. Riot commissions are not the authoritative program planners for a community torn by crisis and harvesting the fruits of past social injustice. Neither are they accorded the status that might accrue to them by virtue of the prestige of individual

commissioners or the expertise that they command. Rather, starting from the myth that riot commissions will provide authoritative answers to questions of social concern, and that these answers will be widely accepted by politicians who will move to implement them, riot commissions move through a process in which they become just another pressure group among many in the political process. And in influencing that process, their resources are insufficient to prevail in the competition.

The allegation that commissions have repeatedly come to the same analysis, recommended similar programs, and failed to produce action is true, but as criticism it is misdirected. It is not the commissions themselves to which one must look to understand the "Alice-in-Wonderland" atmosphere that Kenneth Clark perceived. One must look to the political process itself—that greater Wonderland in which riot commissions play only a marginal role.

July/August 1969

FURTHER READING SUGGESTED BY THE AUTHORS:

From Race Riot To Sit-In: 1919 and the 1960's by Arthur T. Waskow (Garden City: Doubleday, 1966) is an historical and comparative study of race riots of the World War I period with particular emphasis on the Chicago Commission on Race Relation's investigation of the 1919 Chicago race riot.

Racial Crisis in America: Leadership in Conflict by Lewis Killian and Charles Grigg (Englewood Cliffs: Prentice-Hall, 1964) is a creative analysis of functions performed by racial conflict and of limitations inherent in Southern biracial committees.

Race Riot at East St. Louis: July 2, 1917 by Elliott M. Rudwick (Cleveland, Ohio: Meridian Books, 1966) is a thorough study of a major race riot including analysis of four separate investigations into riot causes and remedies.

This article is part of a larger study of the political impact of riots on American cities. The study has been supported by the Harvard-M.I.T. Joint Center for Urban Studies, by *Trans*-action, and by the Institute for Research on Poverty, University of Wisconsin.

The Wallace Whitelash

SEYMOUR MARTIN LIPSET/EARL RAAB

The American Independent Party of George C. Wallace brought together in 1968 almost every right-wing extremist group in the country, and undoubtedly recruited many new activists for the rightist cause. Today many of the state parties organized under his aegis have formal legal status and have announced that they intend to nominate candidates for state and local office during the next few years in an effort to build the party. George Wallace himself has sent out a clear signal that he has plans for the future. He has begun to mail the *George Wallace Newsletter* monthly to a mailing list of over one million names which had been assembled during the election. The old address for Wallace activities was Box 1968, Montgomery, Alabama. It is now Box 1972.

The effort to maintain and build the party, however, faces the perennial problem of ideological extremist movements—splits among its supporters. Even during the 1968 campaign, sharp public divisions over local vs. national control occurred in a number of states, usually because complete control over the finances and conduct of the party's work was kept in the hands of coordinators directly appointed by Wallace and responsible to the national headquarters in Montgomery. In some states, two separate organizations existed, both of which endorsed the Wallace candidacy but attacked each other as too radical. Since the 1968 election, two competing national organizations have been created, and again each is attacking the other as extremist.

The group directly linked to Wallace has had two national conventions. The first, held in Dallas in early February, attracted 250 delegates from 44 states and set up a group known as The Association of George C. Wallace Voters. The Dallas meeting was attended by a number of top Wallace aides, including Robert Walter, who represents Wallace in California; Tom Turnipseed, a major figure in the Wallace presidential effort since it started; Dan Smoot, the right-wing radio commentator; and Kent Courtney, the editor of the *Conservative Journal*. The same group met again on May 3 and 4 in Cincinnati, and formally established a new national party to be called The American Party. A Virginian, T. Coleman Andrews, long active on the ultraconservative front, was chosen as chairman. Wallace gave his personal blessing to the new party and its officers. One of his Montgomery aides, Taylor Hardin, who maintains a national office with 20 employees in Montgomery, indicated that the party would have a considerable degree of "central control."

The competing national group met in Louisville on February 22, 1969, and established a new national conservative party to be composed largely of autonomous state parties.

As if to emphasize the extent to which it fostered local control, this organization called itself "The National Committee of the Autonomous State Parties, known as the American Independent Party, American Party, Independent Party, Conservative Party, Constitutional Party." This group, or constellation of groups, was united in its opposition to domination by Wallace and his Montgomery aides. Although the former candidate received compliments at the convention, the delegates were much more concerned with building a movement that was not limited to his supporters in 1968. The national chairman of the new group, William K. Shearer of California, editor of the *California Statesman*, had already broken with Wallace during the campaign on the issue of local autonomy. At the Louisville convention, Shearer said:

> Governor Wallace has not shown any interest in a national party apart from a personal party. A candidate properly springs from the party and not the party from the candidate. The party should not be candidate-directed. While we have great respect for Mr. Wallace, we do not think there should be a candidate-directed situation. We want our party to survive regardless of what Mr. Wallace does.

The Shearer group also appears to be more conservative on economic issues than the Wallace-dominated one. During the convention, Wallace was criticized for being "too liberal" for his advocacy during the campaign of extended social security and farm parity prices.

The leaders of each faction claim that the other includes extremists. Robert Walters attacked Shearer's group as composed of "radicals and opportunists" and as having "a pretty high nut content." Shearer, on the other hand, has said that he finds many in the Wallace-dominated party "not too savory."

The publications of the competing groups indicate that each is supported by viable segments of the 1968 party. The Shearer National Committee, however, is clearly much weaker financially, since the Wallace national group retained a considerable sum from the 1968 campaign for future activities. It is also unlikely that they can attract many Wallace voters against the opposition of the candidate. The competition for support, however, does give each group an immediate function; and both national organizations appear to be busy holding state and local conventions designed to win over those who were involved in the presidential campaign.

It is difficult to tell how much support the American Party retains. Early in 1969 the party ran a candidate in a special election for Congress in Tennessee's Eighth District. Wallace ran first in this district in the presidential race, but the A.I.P. congressional candidate, William Davis, ran a bad second to the Democrat. The A.I.P. secured 16,319 votes (25 percent) in the congressional race, compared to 32,666 for the Democrat and 15,604 for the Republican. Wallace himself took an active part in the campaign, making speeches for Davis, but he was clearly unable to transfer his presidential support to his follower.

While Davis's showing in Tennessee was fairly respectable, another A.I.P. by-election candidate, Victor Cherven, who ran for the state senate in Contra Costa County in California in late March, secured only 329 out of the 146,409 votes cast. Cherven even ran behind two other minor party nominees. In mid-June, in a by-election for a seat in the California assembly from Monterey, an A.I.P. candidate, Alton F. Osborn, also secured an insignificant vote, 188 out of 46,602. The first effort to contest a congressional seat outside the South failed abysmally, when an American Party candidate in a Montana by-election received half of 1 percent of the vote, 509 out of 88,867 ballots on June 25. Election day, November 4, 1969, produced the best evidence of the inability of the Wallace followers to develop viable local parties. In Virginia, a state in which Wallace had secured 322,203 votes or 23.6 percent in 1968, both rightist parties ran candidates for governor. Dr. William Pennington, the gubernatorial nominee of the Andrews-Wallace American Independent Party obtained 7,059 votes, or .8 percent of the total; and Beverly McDowell, who ran on the Conservative Party ticket of the Shearer segment of the movement, did slightly better, with 9,821 votes, or 1.1 percent of the electorate. Pennington's and McDowell's combined total in 1969 only equalled 5 percent of Wallace's vote in Virginia.

But if Wallace's strength cannot be transferred to local and state candidates, most of it still remains with him on the level of national politics. The Gallup Poll, which chronicled George Wallace's rise in popularity through 1967 and 1968, has continued to examine his possible strength in a future presidential contest. In three national surveys in April, July and September, samples of the electorate were asked how they would now vote in a contest between Nixon, Edward Kennedy and Wallace. Nixon appeared to have gained from both parties, as compared with the 43 percent he received in the 1968 election. His support remained consistently high, 52 percent in April, 52 in July, and 53 in September. Kennedy's backing fluctuated more, 33, 36, 31, as contrasted with the 43 percent that Humphrey had secured. Wallace also dropped, securing 10, 9, and 10 percent in the same three polls. Thus, he lost about a quarter of his support during 1969, but still retains a respectable following for a new campaign. Wallace's social base remains comparable to that which backed him in the election, and he remains a major force in the South, where he pulls 25 percent of the choices as compared with 5 percent in the rest of the country.

Who *did* support George Wallace in 1968? A detailed answer to that question will perhaps tell us more than anything else about his chances for the future, as well as about the potentiality of right-wing extremism in America.

Election Day results confirmed the basic predictions of the preelection opinion polls. George Wallace secured almost ten million votes, or about 13.5 percent of the total voting electorate. He captured five states with 45 electoral votes, all of them in the Deep South: Mississippi, Georgia, Alabama, Louisiana and Arkansas. With the exception of Arkansas, which had gone to Johnson in 1964, these were the same states Barry Goldwater won in that year. But Wallace lost two states carried by Goldwater—South Carolina, the home state of Nixon's southern leader, the 1948 Dixiecrat candidate Strom Thurmond, and Arizona, Goldwater's home state.

Since the support for Wallace seemingly declined considerably between early October and Election Day, falling from about 21 percent to 13 percent, an analysis of his actual polling strength is obviously important. Fortunately, the Gallup Poll conducted a national survey immediately after the election in which it inquired both how respondents voted, and whether they had supported another candidate earlier in the campaign. The data of this survey were made available by the Gallup Poll for our analysis. They are particularly useful since it would appear that most voters who had supported Wallace, but shifted to another candidate, did report this fact to Gallup interviewers. Thirteen percent indicated they had voted for Wallace, while another 9 percent stated that they had been for him at an earlier stage in the campaign.

From the national results among whites, it is clear that the data are heavily influenced by the pattern of support in the South. Wallace's voters were most likely to be persons who did not vote in 1964, or who backed Goldwater rather than Johnson. The pattern of an extremist party recruiting heavily from the ranks of nonvoters coincides with the evidence from previous extremist movements both in this country and abroad. Wallace also clearly appealed to those in smaller communities, and his strength was greatest among those with the least education. With respect to income, his backers were more likely to come from the poorer strata than the more well-to-do, although he was slightly weaker among the lowest income class—under $3,000— than among the next highest. He was strongest among those in "service" jobs, a conglomerate which includes police, domestic servants and the military. Of the regular urban occupational classes, his support was highest among the unskilled, followed by the skilled, white collar workers, those in business and managerial pursuits, and professionals, in that order. The number of farmers voting for Wallace was relatively low, a phenomenon stemming from differences between farmers in the South and in the rest of the country. Among manual workers, Wallace was much weaker with union members than nonunionists.

The vote behavior with respect to other factors also corresponds in general to preelection predictions. Wallace was backed more heavily by men than by women, a pattern characteristically associated with radical movements, whether of the left or right. Surprisingly, young voters were more likely to prefer him than middle-aged and older ones, with the partial exception that voters in the 25- to 29-year-old category were a bit more likely to prefer Wallace than the

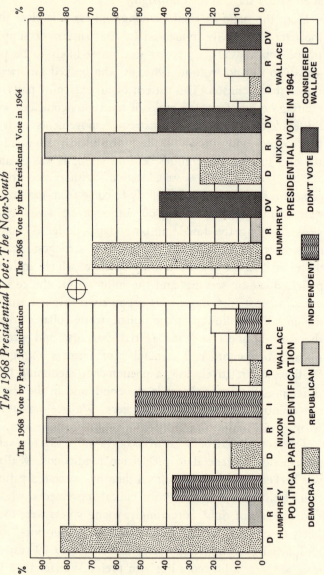

The 1968 Presidential Vote: The Non-South

The 1968 Vote by Party Identification

The 1968 Vote by the Presidental Vote in 1964

POLITICAL PARTY IDENTIFICATION

PRESIDENTIAL VOTE IN 1964

DEMOCRAT   REPUBLICAN   INDEPENDENT   DIDN'T VOTE   CONSIDERED WALLACE

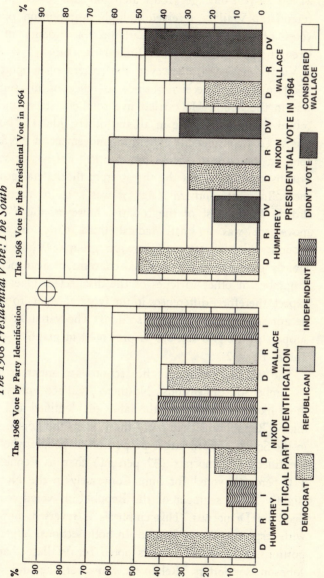

The 1968 Presidential Vote: The South

The 1968 Vote by Party Identification

The 1968 Vote by the Presidental Vote in 1964

HUMPHREY   NIXON   WALLACE
D R I   D R I   D R I
POLITICAL PARTY IDENTIFICATION

HUMPHREY   NIXON   WALLACE
D R DV   D R DV   D R DV
PRESIDENTIAL VOTE IN 1964

DEMOCRAT   REPUBLICAN   INDEPENDENT

DIDN'T VOTE   CONSIDERED WALLACE

21- to 24-year-old age group. Religion also served to differentiate: Wallace received a higher proportion of the votes of Protestants than Catholics, a product of his strength in the predominantly Protestant South.

Viewed nationally, however, the pattern of support for Wallace is a bit deceiving since so much of his support was in the South. He carried five southern states and received a substantial vote in all the others, plus the border states. To a considerable extent, his movement in the South took on the character of a "preservatist" defense of southern institutions against the threat from the federal government. In most southern states, it was a major party candidacy. In the rest of the country, however, the Wallace movement was a small radical third party, organized around various extreme right-wing groups. While it obviously gave expression to racial concerns, it also included a number of other varieties of the disaffected. One would expect, therefore, differences in the types of voters to whom he appealed in the different sections. The variation in his support in the two sections is presented in graphs 1-4 and Tables 1 and 2.

The variations between the sections are apparent along a number of dimensions. Northern Wallace voters were more likely to come from the ranks of identified and committed Republicans than were those from the South. Thus in the South, a much larger proportion of people who were identified as Democrats (37 percent) than as Republicans (10 percent) voted for him. Conversely in the North, a slightly larger segment of the Republicans voted for him than did Democrats. This emphasis is reversed, however, with respect to the 1964 vote. In both sections, larger proportions of Goldwater voters opted for Wallace than did Johnson supporters. Relatively, however, he did better among the southern Goldwater voters. The seeming contradiction may be explained by the fact that Wallace did best among "independents," and that there were proportionately many more independents in the South than in the North. Southern independents presumably are people who have opted out of the Democratic party toward the right, many of whom voted for Goldwater in 1964 and Wallace in 1968. His greatest support, both North and South, of course, came from the ranks of those who did not vote in 1964. Almost half of the southern nonvoters in the 1964 election who voted in 1968 chose Wallace.

The effect of the social stratification variables were relatively similar in both parts of the country. In general, the better educated, the more well-to-do, and those in middle-class occupations were less likely to vote for Wallace than voters in the lower echelons.

As far as religion is concerned, nationally Wallace appeared to secure more support among Protestants than Catholics, but a sectional breakdown points up the fact that this was an artifact of the relatively small Catholic population in the South. Outside of the South, Wallace secured more support from Catholics than from Protestants. The pattern appears to be reversed in the South, but the number of Catholics in the sample is too small to sustain a reliable estimate. What is perhaps more significant than the Catholic-Protestant variation is the difference among the Protestant denominations. Wallace's greatest backing, North and South, came from Baptists, followed by "other," presumably mainly fundamentalist sects which have a history of disproportionately backing right-wing groups. Wallace, after all, became the protector of the "southern way of life" and the status of those who bear it, not only for southerners, but for southern migrants to the North. This, apart from education, is one significance of the disproportionate support of Wallace by northern Baptists.

As noted earlier, perhaps the most surprising finding of the polls was the consistent report by Gallup, Harris and the Michigan Survey Research Center that youth, whether defined as 21 to 24 or 21 to 29 years old, were more favorable to the third-party candidate than those in older age groups. Two special surveys of youth opinion also pointed in this direction. One was commissioned by *Fortune* and carried out by the Daniel Yankelovich organization among 718 young people aged 18 to 24 in October 1968. It revealed that among employed youth 25 percent were for Wallace, as compared to 23 for Humphrey, 31 for Nixon and 15 without a choice. Among college students, Wallace received 7 percent of the vote. A secondary analysis of this survey indicated that class and educational level differentiated this youth group as well. Thus 31 percent of young manual workers who were the sons of manual workers were for Wallace, as contrasted with but 6 percent among nonmanuals whose fathers were on the same side of the dividing line. A preelection survey by the Purdue Opinion Poll among a national sample of high school students, reported that Wallace had considerable strength among them as well: 22 percent, backing which came heavily from members of southern, and economically less affluent families.

This "shift to the right" among youth had first been detected among young southerners. Although various surveys had found a pattern of greater youth support for integration in the South during the forties and fifties, by the 1960's this finding had been inverted, according to two NORC polls reported by Paul Sheatsley and Herbert Hyman. They suggested that southern youth who grew up amid the tensions produced by the school integration battles reacted more negatively than the preceding generations who had not been exposed to such conflicts during their formative political years. And as the issue of government-enforced integration in the schools and neighborhoods spread to the North, white opinion in central city areas, which are usually inhabited by workers, also took on an increased racist character.

What has happened is that increasing numbers of white young people in the South and in many working-class districts of the North have been exposed in recent years to repeated discussions of the supposed threats to their schools and communities posed by integration. They have been reared in homes and neighborhoods where anti-Negro sentiments became increasingly common. Hence, while the upper-middle-class scions of liberal parents were being radicalized to the left by civil rights and Vietnam war issues, a sizeable segment of southern and northern working-class youth were being radicalized to the right. The consequence of such polarization can be seen in the very different behavior of the two groups in the 1968 election campaign.

The indications that the Wallace movement drew heavily among youth are congruent with the evidence from various studies of youth and student politics that suggests young people are disposed to support the more extreme or idealistic version of the politics dominant within their social strata. In Europe, extremist movements both of the right and left have been more likely to secure the support of the young than the democratic parties of the center. Being less committed to existing institutions and parties than older people, and being less inured to the need to compromise in order to attain political objectives, youth are disproportionately attracted to leaders and movements which promise to resolve basic problems quickly and in an absolute fashion.

1968 PRESIDENTIAL VOTING IN THE NON-SOUTH BY %

	Voted for			Consid-ered Wallace	Total Wallace Symp.
	Humphrey	Nixon	Wallace		
OCCUPATION					
Non-manual	42	53	5	5	10
Manual	49	42	9	13	22
Union family	57	34	9	16	25
Nonunion	39	52	9	8	17
EDUCATION					
Grade school or less	53	40	7	10	17
High school or less	43	49	7	9	17
Some college	43	52	5	4	9
INCOME					
less than $3,000	41	53	5	5	11
$3,000-$6,999	46	44	10	9	19
$7,000-$9,999	42	52	6	11	17
$10,000-$14,999	46	47	6	8	14
$15,000 plus	39	58	3	7	10
RELIGION					
Roman Catholic	53	39	8	9	17
Jewish	87	13	—	3	3
Protestant	34	53	6	10	15
Baptist	33	51	16	10	25
Methodist	32	65	3	10	13
Presbyterian	28	68	5	11	15
Lutheran	43	54	3	6	9
Episcopal	40	61	—	5	5
Others	31	59	9	13	22
SIZE OF PLACE					
Rural	37	56	7	11	20
2,500-49,999	43	52	5	6	11
50,000-499,999	44	51	6	5	10
500,000-999,999	46	45	9	6	16
1,000,000 plus	50	44	7	8	15
AGE					
21-25	54	34	13	7	20
26-29	35	54	11	6	17
30-49	43	49	8	14	22
50 plus	43	53	3	5	8
SEX					
Men	43	48	9	11	20
Women	45	51	5	6	11

1968 PRESIDENTIAL VOTING IN THE SOUTH BY %

	Voted for			Considered Wallace	Total Wallace Symp.
	Humphrey	Nixon	Wallace		
OCCUPATION					
Non-manual	22	57	22	14	36
Manual	14	33	53	6	59
Union family	30	30	40	5	45
Nonunion	8	34	58	6	64
EDUCATION					
Grade school or less	23	28	49	8	57
High school or less	21	42	36	11	48
Some college	19	60	21	10	31
INCOME					
less than $3,000	27	30	43	8	51
$3,000-$6,999	18	39	44	5	48
$7,000-$9,999	17	42	42	12	54
$10,000-$14,999	23	63	15	13	28
$15,000 plus	24	62	15	15	29
RELIGION					
Roman Catholic	47	29	24	6	29
Jewish	—	—	—	—	—
Protestant	18	46	36	10	46
Baptist	13	43	45	11	56
Methodist	22	43	35	5	40
Presbyterian	10	76	14	14	29
Lutheran	—	—	—	—	—
Episcopal	—	—	—	—	—
Others	21	25	45	7	52
SIZE OF PLACE					
Rural	17	38	45	4	49
2,500-49,999	21	43	36	8	44
50,000-499,999	23	52	25	9	33
500,000-999,999	31	58	12	3	15
1,000,000 plus	—	—	—	—	—
AGE					
21-25	—	—	—	—	—
26-29	26	37	37	5	42
30-49	14	52	34	8	41
50 plus	26	41	33	10	43
SEX					
Men	24	39	37	11	48
Women	18	51	31	8	39

So much for those who actually voted for Wallace. Equally significant are those who supported Wallace in the campaign but didn't vote for him. Presumably many who shifted from Wallace did so because they thought he could not win, not because they would not have liked to see him as president. This is the uneasiness of the "lost vote." There is also the "expressive" factor, the votes in polls which do not count. Casting a straw vote for Wallace was clearly one method of striking a generalized note of dissatisfaction in certain directions. But since total considerations take over in the voting booth, the nature of the defections becomes one way to measure these dissatisfactions in various quarters. On another level, there is the factor of the social reinforcements that may or may not exist in the voter's milieu and are important for the ability of a third-party candidate to hold his base of support under attack.

In general, Wallace lost most heavily among groups and in areas where he was weak to begin with. Individuals in these groups would find less support for their opinions among their acquaintances, and also would be more likely to feel that a Wallace vote was wasted. In the South, however, almost four-fifths of all those who ever considered voting for Wallace did in fact vote for him. In the North, he lost over half of his initial support: only 43 percent of his original supporters cast a ballot for him. Similarly, Baptists and the small "other" Protestant sects were more likely to remain in the Wallace camp than less pro-Wallace religious groups.

There were certain significant differences in the pattern of defections with respect to social stratification. In the South, middle-class supporters of Wallace were much more likely to move away from him as the campaign progressed. He wound up with 90 percent of his preelection support among southern manual workers, and 61 percent among those in nonmanual occupations. In the North, however, Wallace retained a larger proportion of his middle-class backers (52 percent) than of his working-class followers (42 percent).

The data from the Gallup survey suggest, then, that the very extensive campaign of trade union leaders to reduce Wallace support among their membership actually had an effect in the North. Almost two-thirds (64 percent) of northern trade union members who had backed Wallace initially *did not* vote for him, while over half of those southern unionist workers (52 percent) who had been for him earlier voted for him on Election Day. A similar pattern occurred with respect to the two other measures of stratification, education and income. Wallace retained more backing among the better educated and more affluent of his northern supporters, while in the South these groups were much more likely to have defected by Election Day than the less educated and less privileged.

The variations in the class background of the defectors in the different sections of the country may be a function of varying exposures to reinforcing and cross-pressure stimuli in their respective environments. On the whole we would guess that middle-class Wallace supporters in the North came disproportionately from persons previously committed to extreme rightist ideology and affiliations. Wallace's support among the northern middle-class corresponds in size to that given to the John Birch Society in opinion polls. If we assume that most people who were pro-Birch were pro-Wallace, then presumably Wallace did not break out of this relatively small group. And this group, which was heavily involved in a reinforcing environment, could have been expected to stick with him. In the South, on the other hand, he began with considerable

middle-class support gained from people who had been behind the effort to create a conservative Republican party in
that section. The majority of them had backed Barry
Goldwater in 1964. This large group of affluent southern
Wallace-ites encompassed many who had not been involved in extremist activities. And it would seem that the
efforts of the southern conservative Republicans (headed by
Strom Thurmond) to convince them that a vote for Wallace
would help Humphrey were effective. Conversely, among
northern manual workers, an inclination to vote for Wallace placed men outside the dominant pattern within their
class.

Which of the other two candidates the Wallace defectors voted for clearly depended on background. Three-
fifths of those who shifted away from Wallace during the
campaign ended up voting for Nixon. But those Wallace
backers who decided to vote for one of the major party
candidates almost invariably reverted to their traditional
party affiliation. The pattern is even clearer when southern
Democrats are eliminated. Among the 29 northern Democrats in our sample who defected from Wallace, 90 percent
voted for Hubert Humphrey. Humphrey recruited from
among the less educated and poorer Wallace voters, Nixon
from the more affluent and better educated.

The pattern of shifting among the Wallace voters points
up our assumption that Wallace appealed to two very different groups: economic conservatives concerned with re-
pudiating the welfare state, and less affluent supporters of
the welfare state who were affected by issues of racial integration and "law and order." As some individuals in
each of these groups felt motivated to change their vote,
they opted for the candidate who presumably stood closer
to their basic economic concerns. The data also point up
the difficulty of building a new movement encompassing

people with highly disparate sentiments and interests.

After specifying what kinds of groups voted for whom, the most interesting question still remains, especially with respect to deviant and extremist political movements such as Wallace's: What creates the differentials within each of these groups? Why, in other words, do some members of a group vote for a particular candidate, but not others? Quite clearly, members of the same heuristic group or class may vary greatly in their perception of the world, and will therefore differ as to political choice. Since candidates do differ in their ideology and position on particular issues, we should expect that the values of the electorate should help determine which segments of a particular strata end up voting one way or another.

Data collected by the Louis Harris Poll permit us to analyze the connection between political attitudes and voter choice in 1968. The Harris data are derived from a special reanalysis of the results of a number of surveys conducted during the campaign that were prepared by the Harris organization for the American Jewish Committee. Based on 16,915 interviews, it points up consistent variations. The question that best indicated differing political attitudes among those voting for a given candidate was one in the Harris survey that asked, "Which groups are responsible for trouble in the country?" Choices ranged from the federal government to Communists, students, professors, Jews and others. The relevant responses are presented on the preceding pages.

The findings of the Harris organization clearly differentiate the supporters of the different candidates in 1968 and 1964. On most items, the rank order of opinions goes consistently from right to left, from Wallace to Goldwater to Nixon to Johnson to Humphrey. That is, the Wallace supporters show the most right-wing opinions, while the

Humphrey ones are most left. As a group those who voted for Goldwater in 1964 are somewhat more "preservatist" than the Nixon supporters in 1968. There is, of course, a considerable overlap. Since none of these items bear on attitudes toward the welfare state, what they attest to is the disdain which rightists feel towards groups identified with social changes they dislike.

The Wallace supporters differ most from the population as a whole with respect to their feelings toward the federal government, Negroes, the Ku Klux Klan, and most surprisingly, "ministers and priests." Although Wallace himself did not devote much attention to attacking the liberal clergy, his followers were seemingly more bothered by their activities than by those of professors. Although the electorate as a whole was inclined to see "students" as a major source of trouble, Wallace backers hardly differed from the supporters of the two other candidates in their feelings. As far as we can judge from these results, they confirm the impression that Wallace appealed strongly to people who identified their distress with changes in race relations, with federal interference, and with changes in religious morality. It is of interest that the Wallace supporters in the South and those in the non-South project essentially the same pattern. The southern differential is very slight with respect to blaming Negroes, still slight but higher in blaming clergymen, and higher yet in blaming the federal government.

Fears that Wallace would convert his following into an extraparliamentary influence on the government and terrorize opponents by taking to the streets—fears based on statements that Wallace himself made during the campaign—have thus far proved unwarranted. Wallace seems largely concerned with maintaining his electoral base for

GROUPS RESPONSIBLE FOR THE TROUBLE IN THE COUNTRY BY %

	Fed. Govt.	Communists	Students	Negroes	Ministers and Priests	Jews	Hippies	Police	Professors
Total (16,905)	49	76	55	56	25	6	53	14	29
1968 VOTE									
Wallace (2589)	75	88	57	71	41	10	62	9	36
Humphrey (6476)	34	68	51	46	28	5	49	19	25
Nixon (6436)	54	80	58	61	27	5	54	11	33
1964 VOTE									
Johnson (8838)	40	75	55	52	20	5	52	14	25
Goldwater (4716)	64	81	58	64	35	8	57	9	42
1968 VOTE – SOUTH									
Wallace (1321)	79	90	54	73	43	9	67	8	34
Humphrey (1297)	35	64	51	40	17	8	51	21	22
Nixon (867)	60	84	51	69	36	7	60	12	37
1968 VOTE – NON-SOUTH									
Wallace (1268)	71	86	61	70	38	12	54	9	37
Humphrey (5179)	34	68	52	48	18	5	53	18	25
Nixon (5569)	54	79	59	60	25	4	57	11	32

Source: Table constructed from data presented in a Memorandum to the American Jewish Committee from Louis Harris and Associates dealing with a "Survey on groups responsible for trouble in the country." We are extremely grateful to Mrs. Lucy Davidowicz of the American Jewish Committee for permission to use these analyses.

a possible presidential campaign in 1972. The effort to continue control of the party from Montgomery seems to be dedicated to this end.

The existence of local electoral parties, even those willing to follow Wallace's lead completely, clearly poses a great problem for him. Wallace's electoral following is evidently much greater than can be mobilized behind the local unknown candidates of the American Party. To maintain the party organizations, they must nominate men for various offices. Yet should such people continue to secure tiny votes, as is likely in most parts of the country, Wallace may find his image as a mass leader severely injured. He seems to recognize this, and though concerned with keeping control over the party organization, he has also stressed the difference between the "movement" and the "party," describing the two as "separate entities" which agree on "purposes and aims." Wallace is emphatic about this: "The *movement* will be here in 1972. The *movement* is solvent and it will be active." Speaking at the Virginia convention of the American Party in mid-July of 1969, he said, "A new party ought to go very slow. It ought to crawl before it walks. It ought to nominate a candidate only if he has a chance to be elected." In Tulsa he again warned his followers to move slowly, if at all, in nominating congressional and local candidates. He argued that if he were elected president in the future he "wouldn't have any trouble getting support from Congress, because most of its [major party] members were for the things he's for."

One aspect of the nonparty "movement" may be the reported expansion of the Citizens Councils of America, whose national headquarters is in Jackson, Mississippi. Its administrator, William J. Simmons, helped direct Wallace's presidential campaign in Mississippi, where he received 65 percent of the vote. In June, 1969, Simmons said:

There has been no erosion in Wallace strength. Wallace articulates the hopes and views of over 99 percent of our members. This state is not enchanted with Nixon, and Wallace sentiment is very strong indeed.

He also reported that the Council, mainly concerned with the maintenance of segregation in the schools had expanded "as a result of backlash generated by campus riots and better grassroots organizational work." The impetus of the Wallace campaign also had obviously helped. The Citizens Councils remain one reservoir of future organizational strength for Wallace.

Moreover, Wallace has attempted to maintain his ties to other groups whose members had backed him in 1968. The Birch Society's principal campaign during 1969 has been against sex education and pornography; Wallace has devoted a considerable part of his talks during the year to the subject. In addition he publicly embraced for the first time the ultraconservative "Christian Crusade" of Billy James Hargis by attending its annual convention.

In his speeches and *Newsletter* Wallace has retained the same combination of "preservatist" moralism and populist economic issues that characterized his presidential campaign. On the one hand, he continues to emphasize the issues of "law and order," "campus radicalism," "military failures in Vietnam," and "the need for local control of schools." On the other hand, speaking in Tulsa, one of the principal centers of the oil industry, he called for tax reform that would benefit the little man, adding that "the 27½ percent oil depletion allowance ought to be looked into." He argued that we must "shift the [tax] burden to the upper-class millionaires, billionaires and tax-exempt foundations." Since this kind of rhetoric flies in the face of the deep-dyed economic conservatives among his supporters, such as the Birchers, it is clear that Wallace's cafeteria of appeals still suffers from the same sort of contradictions that characterized it in 1968, contradictions, it might be added, which have characterized most other right-wing extremist movements in American history.

Another problem that Wallace faces comes from supporters who want to build an extremist movement, rather than an electoral organization for one man's candidacy. This can be seen in the activities of an autonomous youth organization, the National Youth Alliance, formed by those active in Youth for Wallace. As of September, 1969, the NYA claimed 3,000 dues-paying members recruited from the 15,000-person mailing list of the Youth for Wallace student organizations. The group has a more absolutist and militant character than either adult party, and it is much more unashamedly racist. Members wear an "inequality button" emblazoned with the mathematical symbol of inequality. Among other things, the Alliance advocates "white studies" curricula in colleges and universities. According to its national organizer, Louis T. Byers, "The purpose of these will be to demonstrate the nature of mankind. The equality myth will be exploded forever." In an article describing its objectives the then-national vice-president, Dennis C. McMahon, stated that NYA "is an organization with the determination to liquidate the enemies of the American people on the campus and in the community." The tone of this pro-Wallace youth group sounds closer to that of classic fascism than any statements previously made by Wallace's associates. As McMahon wrote,

> The National Youth Alliance is an organization that intends to bury the red front once and for all. . . . The NYA is made up of dedicated self-sacrificing young

people who are ready to fight, and die if necessary, for the sacred cause.

. . . Now is the time for the Right Front terror to descend on the wretched liberals. In short, the terror of the Left will be met with the greater terror of the Right. . . .

Tar and feathers will be our answer to the pot pusher and these animals will no longer be allowed to prowl and hunt for the minds of American students.

. . . A bright future full of conquest lies ahead of us . . . Soon the NYA will become a household word and the Left will be forced to cower in the sewers underground as they hear the marching steps of the NYA above them.

The racism of NYA leaders includes approval, if not advocacy, of virulent anti-Semitism. Its national headquarters in Washington distributes literature by Francis Parker Yockey, including his book *Imperium,* which defines Jews, Negroes, Indians and other minorities as "parasites" on the Western world. The five members of its adult advisory board have all been involved in anti-Semitic activities. Two of them, Revilo P. Oliver and Richard B. Cotten, were forced out of the Birch Society because of their overt racist and anti-Semitic views. A third, retired Rear Admiral John Crommelein, ran for president on the anti-Semitic National States Rights Party ticket in 1960; while a fourth, retired Marine Lieutenant General Pedro A. Del Valle, is an officer of the Christian Educational Association, which publishes the overtly anti-Semitic paper *Common Sense.* The fifth member of the board, Austin J. App, former English professor at LaSalle College, is a contributing editor to the anti-Semitic magazine *American Mercury.*

Perhaps most interesting of all the problems that Wallace will have to deal with is the fact that the national chairman of his American Party, T. Coleman Andrews, has publicly advocated the Birch Society's version of that hoary international conspiracy, the historic plot of the Illuminati. The Illuminati, which was an organization of Enlightenment intellectuals formed in Bavaria in 1776, and dissolved according to historical record in 1785, has figured in the conspiratorial theories of assorted American right-wing movements as the insiders behind every effort for religious liberalism, economic and social reform since the 1790s. In recent times, both Father Coughlin, the foremost right-wing extremist of the 1930s, and Robert Welch, the head of the Birch Society, have explained various threats to "the American way" from the French Revolution to the Communist movement, as well as the behavior of most key officials of the government, as reflecting the power of this secret cabal of satanically clever plotters. In a newspaper interview following the establishment of the American party in May, Andrews bluntly announced:

I believe in the conspiratorial theory of History. . . . [The Birch Society has been] responsible, respectable. . . . [R]ecently, the Birch Society has begun to prosper. People are beginning to see that its original theories were right. . . . There is an international conspiracy.

Though George Wallace himself has never publicly stated a belief in the conspiracy of the Illuminati (he prefers to talk about the role of Communists, pseudo-intellectuals and the Council on Foreign Relations) the formal organization of his personally controlled national party is headed by a man who has no such hesitation. On May 26, 1969, Wallace formally sanctioned the American Party as the political arm of the movement and said that if he ran for president again it would be under the American Party's banners.

However, while the pulls towards conspiracy theory and towards ideological racism are evident in the background, the logic of the Wallace-ite movement and its future as a mass movement obviously rest on other foundations. S. M. Miller points out that many had been shocked by "the attraction of George Wallace as a presidential candidate to a large number of union members . . . racism appeared to be rampant in the working class." When the vote came, however, racism seemed to have receded before economic concerns. Their disaffection remains nevertheless. As Miller writes, "About half of American families are above the poverty line but below the adequacy level. This group, neither poor nor affluent, composed not only of blue-collar workers but also of many white-collar workers, is hurting and neglected." It is the members of this group that the Wallace-ite movement must grow on if it is to grow, not out of their ideological racism as much as out of their general sense of neglected decline.

Whether the Wallace movement itself will have returned to full or fuller electoral vigor by 1972 depends on a number of factors which emerge from an examination of America's right-wing extremist past. Determinative—not just for the Wallace movement but for any extremist movement—will be the larger historical circumstances. The disaffection of the white working-class and lower middle-class has been noted; if that disaffection grows, and *at the same time* the pressures of an increasingly disaffected black population increase, the soil will of course be fertile for a George Wallace kind of movement. It is the pressure of the emergent black population that provides an essentially preservatist thrust to the social and economic strains of the vulnerable whites. Whether the major political parties can absorb these concomitant pressures in some pragmatic fashion as they have in the past is another conditional factor, which is also partly dependent on historical development.

Wallace, however, is clearly preparing to use another issue in 1972, the responsibility for American defeat in Vietnam. Like others on the right, he has repeatedly argued that if the U.S. government really wanted to win the war, it could do so easily, given America's enormous superiority in resources and weapons technology. Consequently, the only reason we have not won is political: those who have controlled our strategy consciously do not want to win. But, he argued recently, if it "should be that Washington has committed itself to a policy of American withdrawal, irrespective of reciprocal action on the part of the enemy, in effect acknowledging defeat for our forces, which is inconceivable, we feel that such withdrawal should be swiftly accomplished so that casualty losses may be held to a minimum." And he left on October 30 for a three-week tour of Vietnam and Southeast Asia, announcing that he would run in 1972 if Vietnam were turned over to the Communists "in effect or in substance." Clearly Wallace hopes to run in 1972 on the issue that American boys have died needlessly, that they were stabbed in the back by Lyndon Johnson and Richard Nixon.

In order to do so, however, Wallace must keep his movement alive. As he well recognizes, it is subject to the traditional organizational hazards of such a movement, notably fragmentation, and the ascendancy of overt extremist tendencies that will alienate the more respectable leadership and support. During the year following the election, Wallace has performed as though he understood these hazards well. He has avoided expressions of overt extremism. He has attempted to keep his organization formally separated from the fringe groups and more rabid extremists, even those who were in open support of him. In a letter sent to key Wallace lieutenants around the country, asking about the local leadership that might be involved in the next Wallace campaign, James T. Hardin, administrative assistant to Wallace, carefully emphasized that "perhaps of greatest importance, we would like your opinion as to those who demonstrated neither ability nor capability to work with others and who were, in fact, a detriment to the campaign. . . ."

Whether Wallace can succeed in avoiding the organizational hazards of which he seems aware, and whether historical circumstances will be favorable, is of course problematical. But whether his particular movement survives or not, George Wallace has put together and further revealed the nature of those basic elements which must comprise an effective right-wing extremist movement in America.

December 1969

This article was condensed and substantially rewritten from Chapters 9 and 10 of *The Politics of Unreason: Right-Wing Extremism in America, 1790-1970,* published by Harper and Row in 1970.

NOTES ON CONTRIBUTORS

Richard Berk   "White Institutions and Black Rage"

Lecturer in sociology at Goucher College. Berk is currently study-
ing the relation of black militancy and civil disorders to the actions
of city officials and major institutions.

David P. Boesel   "White Institutions and Black Rage"

Research associate with the Group for Research on Social Policy
at John Hopkins University. Boesel is working toward a Ph.D. in
government from Cornell University.

Bettye K. Eidson   "White Institutions and Black Rage"

Associate professor of sociology at the University of Michigan at
Ann Arbor. Eidson's current activities include a study of community structure and conflict in 15 United States cities.

W. Eugene Groves   "White Institutions and Black Rage"

Member of the group for Research on Social Policy at Johns
Hopkins University. Groves is presently conducting a detailed
analysis of policing in the ghetto, and with Peter H. Rossi is
planning to survey the social conflict arising from drug use on
college campuses.

Terry Ann Knopf   "Sniping—A New Pattern of Violence?"

Research associate at the Lemberg Center for the Study of Violence
at Brandeis University. Knopf has authored *Youth Patrols: An
Experiment in Community Participation* and has written several
articles on press coverage of racial disorders.

Seymour Martin Lipset   "The Wallace Whitelash"

Professor of government and social relations at Harvard University since 1965. Lipset's books include *Agarian Socialism, Political Man, The First New Nation,* and *Revolution and Counter
Revolution.* With others he has also authored *Union Democracy,*
and *Social Mobility in Industrial Society.*

Michael Lipsky   "Riot Commission Politics"

Associate professor of political science at the Massachusetts Institute of Technology. Lipsky is the author of *Protest in City Politics: Rent Strikes, Housing and the Power of the Poor.*

David J. Olson   "Riot Commission Politics"

Assistant professor of political science at Indiana University. Olson has written articles on political violence, social change and executive grievance processes. He is presently completing research on the political impact of riots in American cities.

Tom Parmenter   "Breakdown of Law and Order"

Editor of *Inequality in Education*, the bulletin of the Harvard Center for Law and Education. Parmenter wrote this article while a Russell Sage Fellow at *Trans*-action magazine. He is a former reporter for *Chicago's American* (now *Chicago Today*).

Earl Raab   "The Wallace Whitelash"

·Director of the Jewish Community Relations Council of San Francisco, and has taught at San Francisco State College and the University of California at Berkeley. Raab co-authored *Major Social Problems* and with Seymour Martin Lipset he wrote *Prejudice and Society.*

Lee Rainwater   "Open Letter on White Justice and the Riots"

Professor of sociology at Harvard University and affiliated with the Joint Center for Urban Studies at Harvard and MIT. Among Rainwater's books are, *Moynihan Report and the Politics of Controversy*; *Workingman's Wife: Her Personality, World and Life Style,* and the forthcoming *Behind Ghetto Walls: Black Families in a Federal Slum.* He is a senior editor of *trans*action.

Walter Williams   "Cleveland's Crisis Ghetto"

Deputy director of the Center for Priority Analysis, National Planning Association. Williams' current interests include investigating how modern analytical techniques can be used to develop relevant data for social policy.